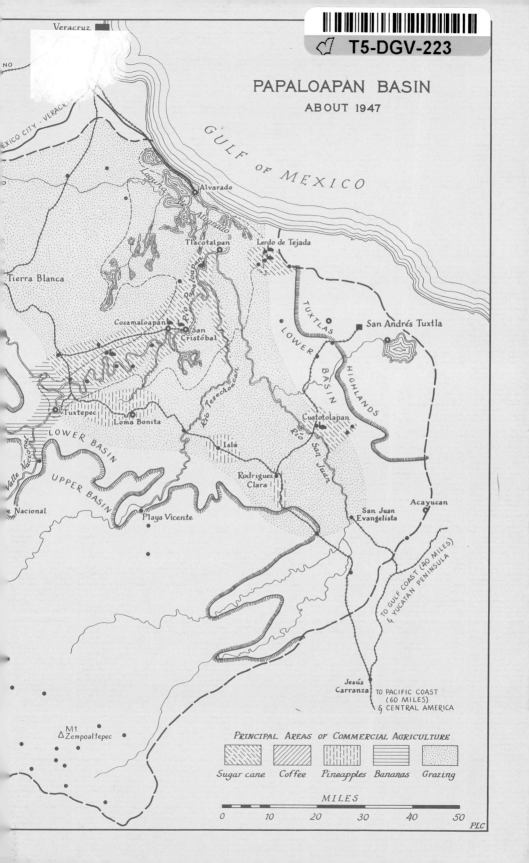

PAPALOAPAN BASIN
ABOUT 1947

Veracruz

GULF OF MEXICO

MEXICO CITY - VERACRUZ

NO

Laguna

Alvarado

Rio Alvarado

Tlacotalpan

Lerdo de Tejada

Tierra Blanca

Rio Papaloapan

Cosamaloapan

San Cristóbal

TUXTLAS

San Andrés Tuxtla

LOWER BASIN

HIGHLANDS

Rio Tesechoacan

Tuxtepec

Loma Bonita

Cuatotolapan

Rio San Juan

LOWER BASIN

Valle Nacional

Isla

UPPER BASIN

Rodriguez Clara

e Nacional

Playa Vicente

San Juan Evangelista

Acayucan

TO GULF COAST (40 MILES) & YUCATAN PENINSULA

Jesús Carranza TO PACIFIC COAST (60 MILES) & CENTRAL AMERICA

Mt. △ Zempoaltepec

PRINCIPAL AREAS OF COMMERCIAL AGRICULTURE

| Sugar cane | Coffee | Pineapples | Bananas | Grazing |

MILES
0   10   20   30   40   50

PLC

THE PAPALOAPAN PROJECT

A Publication of the
FOOD RESEARCH INSTITUTE
STANFORD UNIVERSITY

One of a group of
STUDIES IN TROPICAL DEVELOPMENT

THE PAPALOAPAN PROJECT

Agricultural Development in the Mexican Tropics

Thomas T. Poleman

Stanford University Press

Stanford, California

1964

FOOD RESEARCH INSTITUTE
STANFORD UNIVERSITY

STAFF

STANFORD UNIVERSITY PRESS, STANFORD, CALIFORNIA
LONDON: OXFORD UNIVERSITY PRESS

© 1964 BY THE BOARD OF TRUSTEES OF THE LELAND STANFORD JUNIOR UNIVERSITY

ALL RIGHTS RESERVED

PRINTED IN THE UNITED STATES OF AMERICA

Library of Congress Catalog Card Number: 64-14555

DIRECTOR'S PREFACE

Man has been tempted since antiquity to use the climatic and land resources of the wet regions between the Tropics of Cancer and Capricorn to supply his needs, but his efforts have invariably encountered almost insurmountable obstacles. Only in recent generations has progress in the medical and veterinary sciences, plant pathology, chemistry, and engineering begun to open the disease-, predator-, and pest-infested tropical lowlands to modern civilization and efficient resource use. Even so, problems of extraordinary complexity have to be tackled when new areas of the humid tropics are to be developed, as experience in Africa, Asia, and South America has amply illustrated. Only by trial and error can programs be developed to enable farmers in such regions to compete with well-established producers of similar crops elsewhere, or to attain the level of living in existing settlements of tropical or subtropical regions.

Mexico is richly endowed with natural resources. They comprise minerals, including gas and oil, and a vast expanse of land with a wide range of climates. Their utilization for agricultural development still poses vexing problems. Nevertheless, the Mexican nation has made impressive advances in agriculture in recent decades. This has been accomplished partly by private investment and enterprise and partly by public planning. These advances have been made almost entirely in the subtropical parts of the country, where natural moisture is limited and irrigation yields high returns.

The Papaloapan basin, the site of the project to which this book relates, lies in the humid tropics of Mexico. By comparison with the remarkable progress in the subtropical north, the achievements of the Papaloapan Project during the sixteen years since its inception are very modest. For a number of reasons, the experience, as described and analyzed by Professor Poleman, should be an object lesson to everyone interested in similar undertakings elsewhere in the tropical zone.

Professor Poleman has made a unique and valuable contribution to the subject of economic development in the humid tropics. Not only has he digested the available statistical and documentary evidence about the Papaloapan Project; he has incorporated much information obtained through local inspection and observation and through extensive discussions with administrators and government officials. In his endeavor to find out what actually happened and to put the facts into the proper perspective, he used the methods of empirical analysis and evaluation by standards of comparative economic achievement. These are methods which the Food Research Institute has developed and used in the forty-two years of its work.

The friendly cooperation accorded Professor Poleman by the officials of the Mexican government's Papaloapan Commission while he was associated with the Food Research Institute is hereby gratefully acknowledged.

KARL BRANDT
Director

To the memory of
Raúl Sandoval Landázuri
and what might have been

PREFACE

My interest in the Papaloapan Project was aroused rather by accident. While in Mexico for a few months of travel and study during 1954, I chanced to be invited to join a group who planned to visit the Papaloapan basin. Great things, we were told, were happening: dams were being built, immense tracts were being colonized, new cities were rising. Generally, a wasteland was being transformed into a thriving center of commercial agriculture. Although this description proved a bit wide of the mark, one could not help but be impressed.

For here, after almost a century of talk, a determined effort was being made to develop a section of Mexico's tropical coastland. The implications were far-reaching. If the scheme proved successful, enormous new vistas would open up. The tropical lowlands, historically unpopulated, might well provide the solution to two of Mexico's most pressing problems, rural overpopulation and underproduction. And even if the venture failed to come up to expectations, it would certainly have profound effects. As the first centrally coordinated regional development scheme undertaken in Mexico, its lessons would undoubtedly have a strong influence on subsequent development planning.

Since that first visit in 1954 I have followed the progress of the project as closely as my other activities and my residence some 2,000 miles away have permitted. In October and November 1956 and again during early 1961, the Comisión del Papaloapan kindly permitted me to return for further on-the-spot study. On both occasions I was given unrestricted access to the Commission's files and archives, as well as the opportunity to discuss the project frankly and at length with the Commission's key officials. The value of these visits cannot be overstated. Although the Papaloapan basin is rapidly becoming one of the best-documented regions of Mexico, most information is still to be ferreted out at the source.

I wish to acknowledge a deep debt of gratitude to the many people who have assisted me in the preparation of this study. Foremost among them are the late Ing. Raúl Sandoval Landázuri and Lic. Fernando Rosenzweig Hernandez, who were Vocal Ejecutivo and Director de Economía, respectively, of the Papaloapan Commission during the time of my first two trips to the basin, and Ing. José Ramos Magaña, who was Vocal Ejecutivo in 1961. Without the gracious aid and cooperation of these gentlemen and of many other officials of the Commission, my work truly would have been impossible.

Nor would it have been possible without the encouragement and guidance of my friends and teachers at the Food Research Institute. This study is an outgrowth of my doctoral dissertation; to the members of my Special Committee, Professors V. D. Wickizer, Helen C. Farnsworth, and M. K. Bennett, I owe special thanks. Mr. P. Stanley King, a true innovator in the field of graphic presentation, also was unfailingly helpful. Jane Dobervich drew Map 5; the other maps and charts reflect the talent of Patricia Cedarleaf. Professor Karl Brandt, the Director of the Institute, generously agreed to the publication of the present effort, and Miss Louise Peffer was kind enough to undertake the final editing and to see the manuscript through the press.

As for the statistics used in the study, anyone who has worked with Mexican data is aware of their limitations, including the findings of even the most recent censuses. In the more isolated areas particularly (such as the interior portion of the upper Papaloapan basin), incompleteness of coverage and other inaccuracies continue to confront the researcher with serious conflicts. But as one usually knows where to make allowances, the data are quite serviceable when used selectively and taken as being general, not precise, indicators. Wherever possible, I have tried to avoid employing any of the more questionable statistics, or at least have attempted to point out the probable direction of error.

Unfortunately, the detailed findings of the 1960 Censuses of Agriculture and Population will not be published for several more years; therefore I have been forced to fall back on the figures for 1950, and for the sake of comparability have drawn most comparisons as of that year.

T. T. P.

ITHACA, NEW YORK
MAY 1963

CONTENTS

LIST OF MAPS

LIST OF CHARTS

LIST OF TABLES

THE PAPALOAPAN PROJECT

Chapter 1

INTRODUCTION TO THE PAPALOAPAN PROJECT

The years since the end of World War II have witnessed a number of government-sponsored regional development schemes. One of the oldest and most important of these is the Papaloapan Project, begun by the Mexican government in 1947. Its purpose was, and is, to develop the 17,800-square-mile basin of the Papaloapan River in southeastern Mexico. The course of events to date warrants particularly close investigation because the project represents the first major attempt in recent times to stimulate development in Mexico's—and for that matter in Latin America's—humid tropical regions. These regions make up about 20 per cent of Mexico's land area (Map 1), and are regarded as containing the country's greatest reserves of potentially arable land. Because of isolation, disease, and an unpleasant climatic environment, they have historically supported only a small population and a spotty or very extensive type of agriculture.

ECONOMIC DEVELOPMENT IN THE TROPICS

Numerous forces have combined in the last few decades to focus attention on developing the world's great expanses of sparsely settled humid tropics.[1] Chief among these influences have been the

---

[1] The term "humid tropics" is subject to a considerable range of interpretation. Here it is taken to mean those areas in which the mean temperature of the coolest month does not fall below about 65° F., and in which rainfall is sufficient for non-irrigated agriculture. So defined, it conforms quite closely to those regions which, in terms of the Köppen system of climatic classification, have either a tropical rain forest (Af), a tropical monsoon (Am), or a tropical savanna (Aw) climate. Taken together, these regions embrace about a third of both the world's population and usable land area.

The humid tropical areas of the world may be thought of as falling within one of two broad groupings according to the degree of land utilization encountered and the average density of population supported. Generally speaking, the humid tropics of Asia and the East Indies, with roughly a quarter of the world's people and less than a tenth of its usable land area, are intensively exploited and heavily populated,

MAP 1.—MEXICO: HUMID TROPICAL REGIONS*

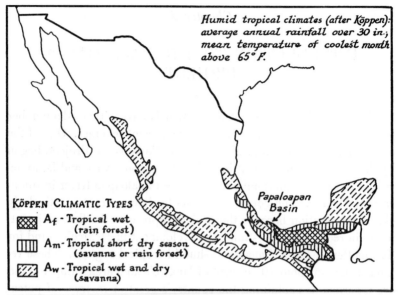

* Adapted from Luis Echeagaray Bablot, "Comentario," in Instituto Mexicano de Recursos Naturales Renovables, *Mesas redondas sobre problemas del trópico mexicano* (México, D. F., 1955), p. 267.

rapid rate of population growth in African and Latin American countries whose boundaries include such areas, and the growing recognition that continuing improvements in material well-being are an essential ingredient of political stability. Though they make up fully a quarter of the world's usable land surface, most of these regions have been exploited to only a fraction of their presumed capabilities. For the many emerging countries in which they lie, their development has come more and more to be a fundamental political and economic necessity.

---

whereas the remaining regions (chiefly situated in Africa and the Americas), with approximately a quarter of the usable land area but less than a tenth of the population, are extensively utilized and thinly settled. Although there are numerous exceptions to this broad categorization, it is to the non-Asian areas that one typically refers when speaking of the "sparsely populated" humid tropics, and it is to these regions that I here refer. (For a generalized map of the humid tropics and a discussion of the contrasts between the Asian and non-Asian components, see *1*, pp. 1–5.)

Economic development suggests different things to different people. Basically, however, it is the process whereby a people come to use the resources available to them in such a way that a sustained increase in output per capita will result. It is thus a relative thing, with its course in any given instance determined by a variety of factors. In many less developed areas, "development" is frequently taken to mean "industrialization." But if a high degree of industrial progress may properly be viewed as a logical end objective for much of the underdeveloped world, only in a few instances does industrialization per se represent a feasible or desirable immediate goal. If the world's underdeveloped regions are considered according to the current character of their economies, only in a distinct minority of cases has the agricultural base evolved sufficiently to warrant a program devoted exclusively to industrialization.

And so it is with the sparsely settled humid tropics. With economies that are overwhelmingly agricultural, populations with but a rudimentary level of education, and abundant supplies of land as their chief resource, development for them must hinge for years to come on the expansion of agricultural production.

Despite at least a century of Western domination, agriculture in the sparsely populated humid tropics remains for the most part a primitive operation. Except for a small commercial fringe composed of plantation-type units and associated smallholders, output continues to be almost entirely in the hands of subsistence peasant growers. Although clearly irreconcilable with rapid growth, this hand-to-mouth structure persists for good reason. It contains all the seeds for its own perpetuation: a poverty of capital resources, ignorance of improved techniques and implements, and isolation from outside influences and means of learning.

This lack of dynamism is aggravated by the physical environment in which the tropical farmer must wrest his living. The combination of heat and humidity affects nearly every phase of his agriculture, sometimes beneficially, but more often detrimentally; thus while it is highly conducive to plant growth, it is also favorable to a multiplicity of pests and diseases and to rapid decomposition and decay. Chiefly because of the effects of rapid decay on tropical soils and their management, farming is studded with apparent conflicts. Soils that produce lush natural vegetation and yield bountiful harvests when initially cleared support crop agriculture for only a few years before decline of fertility and weed growth force the grower to move on. Under the resulting system of shifting cultivation it is deceptively easy for a family barely to subsist, but almost impossible for it to advance unaided. Disease, heat, and, on occasion, inadequate diets sap the worker's energy, while ignorance and poverty hinder attempts to overcome nature's obstacles.

Substantial injections of capital and advanced technology are required if this cycle of stagnation is to be overcome and a region opened to commerce and planted to profitable crops on the scale needed to raise per capita output. Until well into the twentieth century, tropical development was viewed almost exclusively in terms of export-crop production, and most of the necessary investment was directed through private channels into the plantation system of production. Little thought was accorded the peasant grower; peasants could enter the service of the plantation or avail themselves of its facilities where accessible, but otherwise were little affected.

Exclusive reliance on the plantation system proved to have several drawbacks. The advantages and disadvantages of the plantation have been much debated. Suffice it to say that although the system was and is admirably suited as a means for attracting capital and promoting the efficient production of exportable surpluses, the social consequences of its introduction are not necessarily favorable. Furthermore, because the size and impersonal character of the plantation frequently give the appearance of ignoring the needs and individual aspirations of its workers, the system has become a favorite political target. Within the last several decades, as a result, the emphasis of development in most tropical areas has shifted from one of encouraging introduction of estate agriculture to one of facilitating transformation of the subsistence farmer into a commercially active smallholder.

One consequence of this shift has been a progressive expansion in the government's role as supplier of capital, technical knowledge, and organization. A number of factors, not all of which can be asscribed to the growing acceptance of such activities as properly falling within the scope of government, have contributed to this phenomenon. For one, the spread of nationalism in African and Latin American countries has caused investment of private capital of foreign origin to be identified with "semi-colonialism." More generally, however, the movement reflects the unwillingness or inability of private initiative alone to underwrite development of the type and scale contemplated.

The great majority of the numerous governmental development schemes recently initiated have been limited in scope, both with respect to the number of people affected and to the improvements contemplated. Typically, these projects have aimed at introducing some simple advancement to several hundred people at most. Of the more ambitious schemes, designed eventually to aid thousands or hundreds of thousands of farmers, most have also been confined to introducing a single improvement, such as a new crop or improved varieties of traditional crops. A few large-scale projects, however, have proposed to increase output by fundamentally altering the economic and social conditions of an area through a long-term effort.

This last type of project, generally organized for the development of a particular natural region or political subdivision under a decentralized governmental agency, offers certain attractions because of the broadness of its scope and resources. Because the problems of tropical development are manifold and differ considerably from one area to another, such an agency holds a distinct advantage in that it can devote its full attention to the problems prevalent in its particular domain. Then too, because a single agency is empowered to assist the development of a region, it is possible to avoid many of the undesirable features that often characterize the relationship between several governmental organizations operating within the same confines, including administrative clashes, conflicting recommendations, and the resulting adverse effects on public confidence.

But such projects are also subject to serious shortcomings, as the British experience in Africa has amply demonstrated. An ambitious development program, dealing as it does with a little understood subject, must necessarily be vague and therefore fraught with unforeseen problems and opportunities for failure. Resourceful leadership and patient testing are essential if these obstacles are to be overcome. But granted these conditions, this type of scheme is admirably suited as a pilot venture to ascertain both the feasibility of accelerating development in a particular area and the effectiveness of various forms of government assistance. The Papaloapan Project is one such scheme.

THE PAPALOAPAN PROJECT

The Papaloapan Project was begun in 1947 during the first blush of eagerness and optimism following the end of World War II. Unlike most of the other early postwar development schemes, it is still in operation.

The Comisión del Papaloapan, the semi-autonomous agency of the Mexican government charged with the project, was endowed with unusually broad authority. According to its enabling decree, it was granted "full powers to dictate the . . . disposition of industrial, agricultural, and colonization matters insofar as they pertain to the integral development of the Papaloapan basin" (2, p. 181). Water-resource management was heavily stressed in the Commission's planning. The project thus has included more than exclusively agricultural aspects, but because the basin's resources and economy are chiefly agricultural, it has affected that sector primarily.

Since the inception of the project, there have been impressive changes in the Papaloapan basin. No longer outside the main stream of national progress, a substantial part of its area has been opened to progressive influences and is contributing to the expanding national economy. A network of new roads has been constructed; and together with other activities sponsored by the Papaloapan Commission, it has sparked a marked upturn in the region's agricultural output. The project, however, is by no means completed—at least in terms of what the Commission would like to see done. Its officials point to 1976 or thereabouts as the final termination date.

Whether in fact the project will be continued until 1976 is problematical. To an unfortunate extent the scheme has followed the stereotyped pattern of most development projects carried out in Latin America: that of *proyectismo*—of unduly optimistic initial pronouncements succeeded by a rash of expensive errors, declining official interest, and eventual abandonment. This has not been entirely the fault of those who have directed the scheme. To be sure, mistakes have been made; but the formulation and execution of a sound, long-term program have been immeasurably complicated by budgetary instability and by the fact that every six years the Commission has been compelled to adjust its plans to conform to the policies of a new national administration.

At present, the problems confronting the project are particularly acute. Whereas the administrations of Miguel Alemán (1946–52) and Adolfo Ruiz Cortines (1952–58) generally looked on the Commission with favor, the administration of President López Mateos has sharply reduced its powers and budget. In fact, new investment has been virtually suspended since 1961, with most of the budget going for maintenance and basic studies. The time is not inappropriate, therefore, for an accounting of what has been accomplished and what has been learned.

CITATIONS

1 Pierre Gourou, *The Tropical World* (London, 1953).
2 Mexico, Sec. Rec. Hid., Comisión del Papaloapan, *Economía del Papaloapan: Evaluación de las inversiones y sus efectos* (1958).

Chapter 2

THE PROJECT IN PERSPECTIVE:
THE NATIONAL SETTING

The Papaloapan Project is not an isolated instance of intervention by the Mexican government to hasten the development of the nation's agriculture and other economic resources. Rather, it is a single element of a nation-wide effort. In that it was the first major project to be concerned with a region in the humid tropics, however, it marked the beginning of an important new trend. To appreciate the significance of this departure and the meaning of the project to the future development of Mexican farm production, some understanding of the country and the problems confronting its agriculture is useful.

MEXICO AS AN AGRICULTURAL PRODUCER

Mexico is an agricultural country. In spite of several decades of spectacular economic growth its economy remains predominantly agricultural, and will continue to be so in the immediate future. In 1950 about three-fifths of the economically active population was still engaged in farming or allied pursuits. Any broad progress in the economy as a whole is therefore inseparable from agricultural advancement and, indeed, largely dependent upon it.

This dependence must be viewed against an agricultural capability of relatively modest proportions. Although endowed with an extraordinary geographical diversity, Mexico's resources of specific value to agriculture are meager. The country is not only mostly rugged and mountainous; much of its area does not receive enough rainfall to support arable agriculture. Moreover, institutions conducive to the rapid development of the existing productive base have been slow to evolve. Instead of being a dynamic operation,

10

agriculture continues to be dominated by small, semi-subsistence growers whose methods and implements have changed little over time. In short, an unfavorable physical and institutional environment has gone far toward shaping the agricultural problems of Mexico.

Physical Environment

In its physiographic aspect the Republic is composed of a series of clearly defined and sharply contrasted coastal lowlands, interior highlands, and precipitous interjacent escarpments (Map 2). North of the Southern Escarpment, a towering volcanic chain that bisects the country near its center, regions of the latter two types predominate. In this area the surface configuration is dominated by two great mountain ranges, the Sierra Madre Oriental and the Sierra Madre Occidental. Forming the Eastern and Western Escarpments, these ranges parallel the coasts as far north as the United States border and

MAP 2.—MEXICO: PRINCIPAL NATURAL REGIONS*

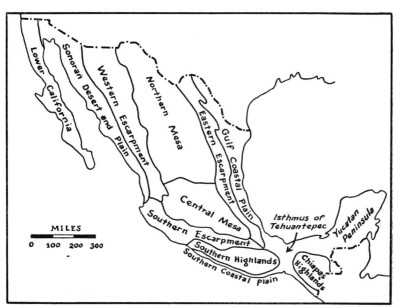

MILES

0   100   200   300

* Adapted from G. McC. McBride, *The Land Systems of Mexico* (New York, 1923), p. 8.

serve to separate relatively narrow coastal plains from an immense inland plateau, or more precisely, series of high intermontane basins. Embracing about a third of the country's area, this great plateau declines from about 8,000 feet near its southern extremity to around 3,000 feet at its northern. It is generally treated as falling into two sub-regions, the Central Mesa and the Northern Mesa. Only in the comparatively minor area south of the Southern Escarpment do lowlands predominate, and even here the Southern and Chiapas Highlands comprise almost half the land area.

Thus most of Mexico is high in elevation and, in spite of its tropical latitude, non-tropical in climate. Decidedly hot temperatures are confined to the coastal lowlands and to the lower reaches of the escarpments; the greater part of the country (about 75 per cent) is relatively temperate or even cool. It is also extremely rugged. About a quarter of the surface has a slope in excess of 25 per cent, and over half in excess of 10 per cent (5, pp. 3–4). Furthermore, of the third that can be considered more or less level, much is located in either the Yucatan Peninsula or the Northern Mesa, where soil and climatic conditions are unfavorable for agricultural operations.[1] Elsewhere, level land is restricted to the narrow coastal fringes, bands along the margins of some of the more important streams, and floors of rather closely confined intermontane basins.

Rugged terrain not only limits the availability of tillable land but presents other obstacles to agricultural development. By impeding the spread of communications, it has fostered a cultural and economic localism which in many regions has only recently begun to be overcome. Only since World War II, for instance, has the Yucatan Peninsula been effectively joined to the rest of the country, and even now many large areas have no modern facilities. Such is the isolation of the inhabitants of the Southern and Chiapas Highlands, especially, that many have no choice but to practice a subsistence agriculture almost entirely outside of the national economy.

The detrimental effects of physiography are nevertheless of sec-

---

[1] As is pointed out below, much of the Northern Mesa is too dry to support non-irrigated cropping. In the Yucatan Peninsula a combination of thin soils and rapid drainage through underlying limestone serves to limit exploitation.

ondary importance when compared with those of climate. Although at least a quarter of the country is too mountainous for agriculture, climate renders additional and even greater expanses unproductive. Lying between 15 and 35 degrees north latitude, Mexico falls under several distinct climatic zones. Generally speaking, the climate north of the Tropic of Cancer is that of the subtropical high pressure zone, and is characterized by very low rainfall (Map 3). To the south the climate is influenced by the intertropical convergence zone and the northeast trade wind, and is favored with higher precipitation. But even here abundant rainfall is not the rule. Although the trade-borne precipitation occasionally reaches as far inland as the western mountains, most is blocked from the interior by the Eastern Escarpment and the Southern Highlands. In the south, therefore, heavy rainfall is restricted to the periphery of the Gulf of Mexico.

Consequently, much of the country is too dry to support agricul-

MAP 3.—MEXICO: AVERAGE ANNUAL RAINFALL*

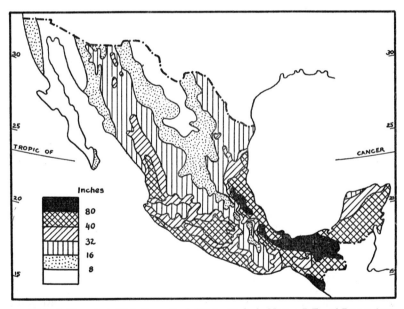

* Adapted from J. A. Vivó, *Geografía de México* (3rd ed., México, D.F. and Buenos Aires, 1953), p. 70.

ture based on field or tree crops. Roughly half of the area receives less than 20 inches annually, and the Ministry of Hydraulic Resources estimates that owing to a low efficiency of rainfall, this portion is almost totally useless to crop production without irrigation (*17*, pp. 20–21).[2] Practically all of the Northern Mesa, the Sonoran Plain, and Lower California are desert, as are segments of the Central Mesa and the Southern Highlands. Although most of the Central Mesa and the southern regions enjoy enough rainfall for one crop yearly, only along the lowlands and escarpments of the Gulf is precipitation truly plentiful.

Fortunately for agriculture, between 80 and 90 per cent of the annual rainfall occurs during the growing season, from May to October. But because the variability of rainfall tends to be related inversely to quantity, agriculture in most of the Republic remains very hazardous. Thus, in the portions of the north and center where mean precipitation would appear adequate, a year-to-year variability relative to the average of as much as 40 to 50 per cent makes farming extremely precarious. Only in the more humid portions of the Central Mesa and the south is the variability of rainfall comparatively low (*26*, pp. 144–54).

Chiefly because of the unfavorable rainfall regime, most of the country is unsuitable for crop agriculture and is either unused or given over to forest or extensive pasturage (Chart 1). In 1949/50, the latest year for which the detailed findings of the decennial Census of Agriculture are available, a mere 10 per cent of the area, or some 20 million hectares, was reported as crop land.[3] And of this, only slightly more than half was actually cropped; the remainder was in

[2] Because the higher average temperatures encourage greater losses through evaporation, the efficiency of a given volume of rainfall in the tropical and sub-tropical latitudes is generally well below that attained in the more temperate zones. Thus much of the world's wheat is produced in relatively cool areas that receive less than 20 inches annually. Nevertheless, it is quite likely that hot-weather crops with especially modest moisture requirements, such as the millets and sorghums, could be successfully grown in portions of the region classified by the Ministry as "useless without irrigation" for the traditional crops of Mexico.

[3] The term "crop land" as defined in the Census of Agriculture refers to land which was cultivated in the year of the census or in any of the previous five years. One hectare equals 2.47 acres.

CHART 1.—MEXICO: LAND UTILIZATION, 1949/50*

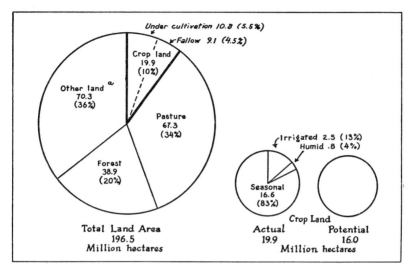

* Based on Mexico, Sec. Econ., Dir. Gen. Estad., *Tercer censo agrícola ganadero y ejidal, 1950. Resumen general* (1956), pp. 28, 31, except for potential crop land, which is based on Armando González Santos, *La Agricultura: Estructura y utilización de los recursos* (México, D.F., and Buenos Aires, 1957), p. 42.

a Includes 50.9 million hectares not censused and presumably non-agricultural.

fallow owing mainly to insufficient moisture. Moreover, about 15 per cent of the crops failed, and three-fourths of this amount was attributable to inadequate precipitation (*13*, p. 2).

Although it is impossible to judge the typicality of the 1949/50 agricultural year because of the dearth of information for non-census years, these data clearly suggest that only a minor portion of even the crop land is "good" in the sense of enjoying a reliable supply of moisture. In fact, the 1950 Census classified less than 20 per cent of the crop land as being "adequately watered" year after year (by either natural or artificial means), and over 80 per cent as dependent on the highly variable seasonal rains. As Frank Tannenbaum has so aptly expressed it, "Mexico is a beautiful place in which to live," but—for the farmer, at least—"a hard place in which to make a living" (*22*, p. 8).

Institutional Environment

Whereas geographical factors set decisive limits to the capabilities of Mexican agriculture, the institutional or human factor largely governs the present nature of production. In this connection, both the country's Indian heritage and three centuries of Spanish domination have left a lasting and generally unfavorable imprint. Prior to the Revolution of 1910, the rural Indian or mestizo was truly Mexico's "forgotten man." When not physically isolated from progressive influences, he was either ignored or exploited by the ruling oligarchy and adopted few of their material and technical advances. As a result, the general techniques of production improved but slightly. Such practices as green manuring, fertilizing, and crop rotation remained virtually unknown, while the wooden plow, machete, and digging stick persisted as the principal agricultural implements.

Ignorance continues to be widespread in rural Mexico. Despite post-Revolutionary efforts to spread learning, the obstacles to development are still immense. In 1950, some 46 per cent of the people over the age of 25 had had no formal training. Of those who had attended school, 90 per cent had been registered for six years or less. The facts that 43 per cent of the population was illiterate in 1950 and that 11 per cent still retained their Indian languages (i.e., spoke both Spanish and some indigenous tongue, or no Spanish at all) give some indication of the educational barriers to be overcome (*10*, pp. 52, 56).

A nucleus of small farmers with a prominent tradition of individual initiative and enterprise on which agricultural progress could be solidly based has been slow to develop. Instead, the history of Mexican agriculture has been primarily one of a struggle between large private latifundia on the one hand and landholding villages on the other. During the colonial period and the first century of independence, output came increasingly under the control of the latifundia, while the importance of the communal Indian village declined. It is estimated that by 1910 at least 90 per cent of rural family heads owned no land, but worked instead as sharecroppers or laborers on large haciendas (*6*, p. 154).

Reaction to this situation, culminating in the 1910 Revolution, brought about a swing to the opposite extreme by creating an agriculture dominated by relatively small units. The chief beneficiary of the reform was the *ejido*, a communally owned, but for the most part individually operated, small farm. In 1949/50 almost half the crop land was held in ejidos, and the average farm holding included only 7.3 hectares of crop land with about four hectares under cultivation (*11*, pp. 13, 31, 245).

The unfavorable consequences of minifundia are compounded in Mexico by the inflexibility of the ejido system as well as by the ignorance and isolation of so much of the rural population. Per capita output and income are necessarily low, and incentives and attractive alternatives for the industrious are few. Although assured of possession of his plot so long as he works it, the enter-prising *ejidatario* can not legally expand his holding, because the sale of ejido land is prohibited. Furthermore, despite the special facilities of the governmental-sponsored Banco Nacional de Crédito Ejidal, access to much needed capital is limited by restrictions pre-venting the mortgaging of land.

Under these conditions it is not surprising that agriculture is largely of a subsistence character and devoted mainly to feeding the population with the cheapest available foodstuffs. Although Mexico is capable of producing a wide range of agricultural commodities, the major fraction of crop land is devoted year after year to the few basic components of the diet of the typical peasant. No less than 60 per cent of the harvested area in 1949/50 was planted to the chief staple, corn (*11*, pp. 31, 85, 88).

POPULATION GROWTH AND AGRICULTURAL PRODUCTION

With an estimated 25.7 million people at mid-century, Mexico is, in a sense, sparsely populated.[4] At that time the average density was only 34 persons per square mile, as compared with 544 and 795 for such heavily populated European states as the United Kingdom and the Netherlands, respectively (*9*, p. 4; *3*, p. 11). But because only about a tenth of the surface area is rated as tillable, the density

[4] By 1960, according to the census of that year, the population had grown to 34.9 million (*12*, p. 12).

per hectare of crop land is quite high. In 1949/50 there were only .8 hectare of crop land and a mere .4 hectare of land under cultivation for every Mexican (*10*, p. 26; *11*, p. 31).

The population is heavily concentrated in the Central Mesa and declines sharply toward the coasts and borders (Map 4). Approximately 50 per cent of the people live in the ten states and Federal District whose boundaries roughly conform to the Central Mesa; and since these states encompass only 14 per cent of the land area, their average density is almost six times that of the rest of the country.

This concentration chiefly reflects the more pleasant living conditions and the relative abundance of crop land owing to a comparatively temperate and moist climatic regime. The Central Mesa is both higher and cooler than the other sections of the Republic, and, except for the southern coastal areas, its rainfall is more plentiful

MAP 4.—MEXICO: DISTRIBUTION OF POPULATION, 1950*

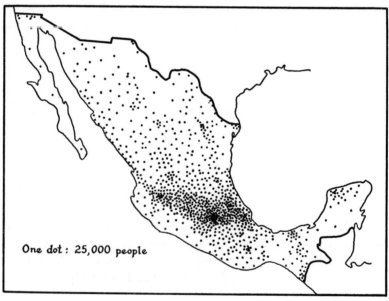

One dot : 25,000 people

* Data from Mexico, Sec. Econ., Dir. Gen. Estad., *Septimo censo general de población. Resumen general* (1953), pp. 26–27.

and uniform. The lack of precipitation in the north renders that area incapable of supporting a large population. Along the coastal plains of the south, on the other hand, heavy rainfall and high temperatures have kept population density low by fostering such obstacles as an unpleasant climatic environment, a comparatively high incidence of human disease in the past, and a *fear* of disease that continues to the present. In brief, the population has historically concentrated in the Central Mesa because it has offered the most favorable environment for human existence.

Until quite recently, the population of Mexico grew very slowly. Variously estimated at between seven and nine million in 1521, it had increased to only 12.5 million by 1895, when the first census was taken (7, p. 41). The decade of revolution from 1910 to 1920 temporarily reversed the moderate upward trend, but since that time the population has surged upward rapidly and at an ever-increasing rate. Between 1922 and 1954 the population more than doubled, and it continues to exhibit one of the most rapid rates of increase in the world. In 1954 the Population Division of the United Nations estimated that by 1980 the country would contain between 48 and 65 million people (23, p. 11). The experience of the last eight years suggests that even the higher figure will prove conservative.

This sudden upsurge may be attributed exclusively to a decline in the mortality rate.[5] Recent improvements in medical and sanitary conditions have brought about a striking drop in this rate, while the birth rate has continued extremely high. For the period 1930–34 the average rate of deaths was 25.6 per thousand, but by 1948–52 it had fallen to 16.6; the birth rate, on the other hand, remained at about 44.5. As a result, the average rate of natural increase, substantial at 18.9 per thousand during the early 1930's, rose to 28.1 during 1948–52 (23, p. 13). Since then, the rate has been even higher: the official estimate for 1956–60 is 34.1 per thousand (12, p. 18).

---

[5] Mexico has attracted only a small volume of immigration, and this has historically been more than offset by permanent emigration from the country (2, pp. 150, 166).

Whether agricultural output has kept pace with the rapid growth in population since the early 1920's and whether it can do so in the future has been much debated. A good bit of the controversy stems from the varying interpretations given official and semi-official production statistics. As in many countries, particularly the less developed ones, Mexican agricultural data are often quite conflicting and in some instances give evidence of being seriously erroneous.

Those who have taken the more pessimistic position and hold that per capita production has not been maintained, most commonly have based their contention on a comparison of official estimates of output for before and after the Revolution. This comparison implies that the general level of production declined drastically during and immediately after the Revolution, and did not again achieve the level attained in 1910 until the early 1940's.[6] It can readily be demonstrated, however, that the pre-Revolutionary data on which this argument rests contain inaccuracies so great as to render them useless as indicators of volume and trend. Consequently, as those who hold the more optimistic view have been quick to point out, it is possible to base judgment only on the data for the post-Revolutionary years. Although the several available series for this period (which for agricultual statistics began in 1925, when the Dirección General de Economía Rural was organized to prepare annual production estimates) also are faulty in some important respects, they may be regarded as much fairer indicators of annual change.

An index derived from one such series, that published by the Mininstry of Industry and Commerce, is plotted in Chart 2. While no claims of accuracy are made to justify selection of this particular series, it should be noted that it agrees fairly closely with the five-year average data drawn up earlier by the highly regarded Combined Working Party of the International Bank (*1*, p. 228). This index suggests that even though the volume of production declined somewhat from 1925 to 1934, it has since more than kept up with population growth and since World War II has increased with singular rapidity.

[6] For one series from which such conclusions could be drawn, see 27, p. 255.

In support of the more optimistic view, there is also evidence that the long-sought goal of self-sufficiency in foodstuffs has all but been achieved. Even allowing for years of severe drought when abnormally large quantities of such staples as corn and beans have to be imported, the United States Embassy has estimated that by the mid-1950's domestic production was able to satisfy about 98 per cent of the country's food requirements. Indeed, if foreign trade is considered, it would appear that Mexican agriculture should be credited with being more than able to take care of domestic food needs at the present level of consumption. Since about 1950, the value of food exports has generally run from two to three times that of imports (*14*, pp. 3, 6).

Nevertheless, these favorable signs should not be taken as suggesting that the agricultural sector is as yet in a position to supply (and the population to afford) the type of diet enjoyed in the economically more advanced countries. Statistical shortcomings still

CHART 2.—MEXICO: POPULATION GROWTH, 1896–1959, AND INDEX OF VOLUME OF AGRICULTURAL PRODUCTION, 1925–1959*

(Logarithmic vertical scale)

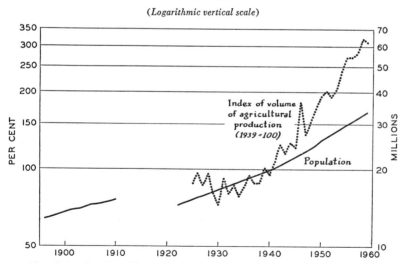

* Population data from Mexico, Sec. Ind. Com., Dir. Gen. Estad., *Anuario estadístico, 1958–1959* (1960), p. 65; agricultural production index from *ibid.*, pp. 481–82, and N. L. Whetten, *Rural Mexico* (Chicago, 1948), p. 255.

prevent any precise determination of per capita supplies of foodstuffs and the composition of the diet, but some insight into their
general nature may be gained from attempts to prepare a food balance sheet for the Republic. According to one such estimate prepared as of 1953 by the United States Department of Agriculture,
apparent daily per capita availability is around 2,500 calories.
While this figure implies a striking increase over that indicated for
the immediate prewar period (of almost 50 per cent if no allowance is made for the wider coverage of recent data), the balance
sheet indicates that the diet, as in other underdeveloped countries,
continues to be heavily composed of the cheaper suppliers of calories. Cereals and sugar contribute roughly 75 per cent of the total
calories available, and corn alone provides approximately half. In
contrast, only a small portion of the diet is made up of fats, animal
proteins, and fruits and vegetables (*28*, pp. 162–63).

But whether production has or has not kept pace with population growth, it is readily apparent that increasingly heavy demands
will continue to be made on Mexico's agricultural capabilities. The
magnitude of these demands, moreover, will in all likelihood be
compounded by a rising level of living. Per capita real domestic
product is thought to have just about doubled between 1939 and
1959, and there appears little indication that it will not continue to
grow (*24*, p. 488). As incomes rise, more people should be able to
afford greater quantities of such preferred foodstuffs as wheat and
animal products, whereas the demand for such cheaply produced
but less desirable staples as corn may well decline.

POPULATION GROWTH AND AGRICULTURAL PRODUCTIVITY

Despite what appears to be a marked upturn in the over-all output
of Mexican agriculture in recent years, productivity as expressed by
the value of output per worker is still extremely low. A rough indication of the seriousness of this situation may be obtained by com-
paring the distribution of the labor force in 1950 with the Combined
Working Party's estimate of net domestic product. This comparison
indicates that the 58 per cent of the economically active population

employed in agriculture accounted for only 20 per cent of total output, while the remaining 42 per cent of the workers contributed 80 per cent (*21*, p. 198). Even though the reliability of the data throws serious doubt on the magnitude of this difference, it is clear that per capita productivity in agriculture lags far behind that achieved in other segments of the economy. There is evidence that this severe disparity has existed since at least 1930 (*15*, p. 22).

Chronic underemployment—reflected by low per capita output and a marginal productivity of labor approaching zero—is most commonly associated with the agricultural sector in underdeveloped economies. It is not, as might be argued for some more advanced countries, the result of inadequate effective demand, but an outgrowth of an insufficient supply of complementary productive factors: land, capital, and advanced technology. Agricultural underemployment is so widespread in Mexico that it has been given the name of *ocio rural*, or "rural idleness" (*16*, pp. 620–31).

While the problem of rural underemployment is nation-wide and by no means restricted to a particular region, it is most acutely felt in the Central Mesa, where the population is heavily concentrated. The value of crop output per agricultural worker in 1949/50 in the states that roughly coincide with this region was only about 650 pesos ($75 at the rate of exchange then prevailing), well below the national average and far below that attained in the irrigated north and humid coastal regions (Chart 3). The reasons for this are clear. Although the proportion of crop land with respect to total area is greater in the Central Mesa than in the remainder of the Republic, the amount available per farm worker is relatively small. Furthermore, because the pressure of population has caused even the most unsuitable land to be brought under cultivation, yields, low throughout the country, are substantially below the national average in the Central Mesa.

Even though a highly significant trend toward industrialization and urbanization has been evident since 1930, the recent population upsurge has tended to impede efforts to increase the per capita productivity of agriculture. The proportion of economically active people engaged in agriculture declined from 70 to 58 per cent between 1930 and 1950, but in absolute terms their number increased by a

CHART 3.—MEXICO: CROP LAND, CROP LAND PER AGRICULTURAL
WORKER, AND VALUE OF CROP OUTPUT PER AGRICULTURAL
WORKER, 1949/50, BY STATISTICAL REGION*

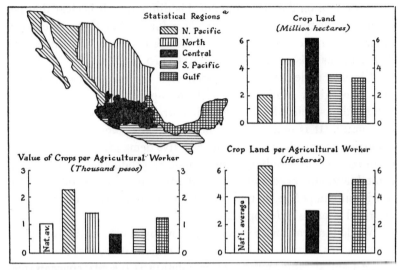

* Based on Mexico, Sec. Econ., Dir. Gen. Estad., *Septimo censo general de población.
Resumen general* (1953), p. 60 and *ibid., Tercer censo agrícola ganadero y ejidal, 1950.
Resumen general* (1956), pp. 31–32, 208–10.
 ᵃ State boundaries have been respected in the formation of statistical regions.

third (*25*, p. 188). Since non-agricultural employment was able to
absorb only two-thirds of the increase in the number of gainfully
occupied during this period, it is reasonable to expect that if the population continues to increase so rapidly, a portion of the new labor force
will have to turn to agriculture. The movement of seasonal farm labor
to the United States may continue to serve temporarily to relieve rural
over-population, but it offers no long-run solution. Manifestly, the
need for more intensive utilization of the tillable area will remain
urgent for many years to come.

Fortunately, the long-run possibilities for improvement are good,
and have only been superficially tapped. As an example of what can
be done, one need only refer to the outstanding results recently
achieved in a program set up to develop and disseminate improved

varieties of seed. Initiated less than 20 years ago with the aid of the Rockefeller Foundation, this program has already brought about a revolutionary upturn in yields. For example, during the program's first decade alone, the limited introduction of hybrid corn varieties in the important Bajío region of the Central Mesa reportedly increased average yields by from 15 to 20 per cent, and even greater increases appear possible (*19*, p. 108). And wider use of commercial fertilizer holds equally promising prospects.

But the introduction of such other beneficial innovations as the rotation of crops, green manuring, and grassland farming is hampered by the small size of the typical holding. Without a transitional margin of surplus land, primitive practices tend to be perpetuated by the need for devoting an entire unit to those crops most necessary for subsistence. Because such a margin can be provided only through a progressive expansion of the tillable area per grower, continued extension of the country's total arable base is also of the utmost importance.

In his evaluation of Mexico's agricultural capabilities (*5*), Armando González Santos estimated that about 36 million hectares could ultimately be brought under cultivation, which indicated the presence of a reserve of some 16 million hectares over and above the 20 million reported as actual crop land in the 1950 Census of Agriculture (Chart 1).[7] But practically all land that can be culti-

[7] Because estimates of the extent of the potentially cultivable area vary widely, it is desirable to justify the use in this study of the one prepared by González Santos. The most widely quoted estimates put forth since 1940 have been those published in the decennial Censuses of Agriculture and one advanced by Adolfo Orive Alba, a former Minister of Hydraulic Resources. The 1940 Census put the area at 7.9 million hectares (*9*, p. 16); the 1950 Census had it as 10.3 million (*11*, p. 31); Orive Alba's 1946 figure put it at 9 million (*18*, pp. 442–43). In comparison with these, González Santos' figure of 16 million, which was calculated as of 1949/50, would appear to be a gross exaggeration. But this is not likely. The decennial Censuses do not purport to cover the entire country, but only that portion which is actually a part of agricultural holdings. They exclude from consideration, therefore, significant segments of the total land area: in 1940 and 1950, 35 and 26 per cent respectively. Orive Alba's estimate can be shown to be similarly incomplete, and appears to refer almost entirely to lands that can be reclaimed for cultivation through some type of water control, either in the form of irrigation, drainage, or flood prevention. González Santos, on the other hand, attempted to estimate the *total* area, including those lands in uncensused regions and those not requiring hydraulic works. For this reason, al-

vated without major investment in irrigation, drainage, and clearance is already being used. Moreover, less than 10 per cent of the potential crop land is situated in the Central Mesa, where the need is most pressing; the great bulk lies in the distant, relatively inaccessible, and thinly settled coastal and northern areas (5, pp. 18–25).

If Mexican agriculuture is to become increasingly productive and remunerative, therefore, considerable outside assistance will be needed. Given the institutional environment within which they operate, Mexican farmers alone cannot be expected to muster the capital resources and technical knowledge required to rapidly convert isolated and inhospitable regions into thriving centers of commercial production.

GOVERNMENTAL AID TO AGRICULTURE

Governmental assistance to agriculture since the Revolution has taken many forms, but, in terms of capital investment, the major emphasis has been on encouraging extension of the cultivable area. Outlays for the promotion of more intensive land utilization such as research and extension services, credit agencies, and the like have been comparatively minor.

Precise delineation of the type and location of the Republic's reserves of potential crop land is, of course, impossible. Nevertheless, one can obtain some insight into their general distribution from the estimates of González Santos. According to his calculations, the total as of the 1949/50 crop year was made up as follows (5, pp. 18–25):

------

though by González Santos' admission his data are crude, one is inclined to accept his view that they more closely reflect reality than do the others.

It should be noted, however, that González Santos does not anticipate that the entire 16 million hectares will ultimately be incorporated into the Republic's agricultural base. The over-all figure of 35.9 million hectares from which it was derived represents a theoretical rather than an expected maximum, and includes both lands of questionable quality and those whose reclamation would defy economic justification. It exceeds by some 5.3 million hectares the maximum which he expects will ultimately be devoted to crop production (5, p. 42).

Million hectares

In the humid tropical regions 10.1
In the arid or semi-arid north (irrigation either essential
  or desirable) 5.3
In the semi-arid Central Mesa (irrigation desirable) 1.4

These estimates suggest that about two-thirds of the area is concentrated in the humid tropical regions of the coastal plains and the south, and that the remainder is situated in the drier portions of the north and center, where irrigation is either essential or desirable for crop agriculture.

Direct governmental efforts to encourage expansion of the cultivated area have been concerned primarily with increasing the amount of land under irrigation in the latter two regions. Since 1939 an average of about 15 per cent of public investment, or almost 80 per cent of all public investment in agriculture, has been allocated to irrigation work (1, p. 194). Betweeen 1926, when the program was begun, and 1961, about 1.4 million hectares of newly irrigated land were opened to cultivation in government projects, and an additional .9 million hectares received improved irrigation facilities (20, between pp. 38–39).

The contribution of this program to the country's agriculture has been immense—far greater, because of the comparatively high productivity of irrigated lands, than area figures alone would suggest. Thus, although the harvested area in federal irrigation districts in 1949/50 made up only 10 per cent of the national total, the value of production amounted to over a third of that of all farms (11, p. 64; 8, p. 249). Owing to the rapid extension of governmental irrigation since 1950, there is every reason to believe that the relative importance of irrigation-district production is now even greater.

But even allowing for the highly speculative character of González Santos' estimates, it is apparent that potentially irrigable land in the drier areas is quite limited and rapidly being exploited. In comparison with its great land area, the possibilities for irrigation in northern Mexico are modest. Few of the rivers in the north flow through or into the mesas; most have their sources in the two coastal escarpments and flow relatively short distances directly into the sea. And many of the streams that do traverse the mesas have cut such deep canyons that they are of little use to agriculture without major works. Between 1940 and 1955 the total irrigated area, including both governmental and private projects, is estimated to have increased by almost 1.5 million hectares. By then, it had become painfully evident that the most favorable dam sites and land surfaces had been utilized, and that further expansion could be had only with substantial increases in costs per hectare (*13*, p. 3).

Long before this stage was reached, awareness of the magnitude of the country's future agricultural requirements had led to growing consideration of the other, more extensive reserve of potential crop land, the presumably productive humid tropical areas of the coasts and the south, where inaccessibility, an unpleasant climatic environment, and fear of disease had generally prevented intensive utilization. But talk was not translated into official policy until 1941, when President Avila Camacho called for a reorientation of governmental asssistance to agriculture (quoted in *4*, p. 190):

> The future of agricultural production lies in the fertile lands of the coasts. A "march to the sea" will relieve congestion in our Central Mesa . . . since the fertility of the coastal belt will make it uneconomical to produce various products in the plateau. But this march requires, as prerequisites, sanitary measures, communications, reclamation and drainage of swamps, and to make such works possible, the expenditure of vast sums. It will be necessary to organize a new type of tropical agriculture, which, because of the nature of the products to be grown, cannot be based on minifundia.

Little more than lip service was paid to this pronouncement during the remaining five and a half years of Avila Camacho's term of office, and it was not until the succeeding administration of Miguel Alemán that steps were taken to implement the new policy. One of the first of these took place when, a few months after assuming office, Alemán created the Papaloapan Commission and charged it with encouraging the development of the Papaloapan basin.[8]

CITATIONS

1 Combined Mexican Working Party, *The Economic Development of Mexico* (International Bank for Reconstruction and Development, Baltimore, 1953).

2 Julio Durán Ochoa, *Población* (México, D.F., and Buenos Aires, 1955).

3 FAO, *Yearbook of Food and Agricultural Statistics, 1951*, part 1 (Rome, 1952).

4 M. R. Gómez, "Producción rural," in Mexico, Sec. Gober., *Seis años de actividad nacional* (1946).

5 Armando González Santos, *La Agricultura: Estructura y utilización de los recursos* (México, D. F., and Buenos Aires, 1957).

6 G. McC. McBride, *The Land Systems of Mexico* (New York, 1923).

7 Mexico, Sec. Econ., Dir. Gen. Estad., *Anuario estadístico, 1953.*

8 Mexico, Sec. Econ., Dir. Gen. Estad., *Compendio estadístico, 1954.*

9 Mexico, Sec. Econ., Dir. Gen. Estad., *México en cifras, 1952.*

10 Mexico, Sec. Econ., Dir. Gen. Estad., *Septimo censo general de población. Resumen general* (1953).

11 Mexico, Sec. Econ., Dir. Gen. Estad., *Tercer censo agrícola ganadero y ejidal, 1950. Resumen general* (1956).

12 Mexico, Sec. Ind. Com., Dir. Gen. Estad., *Compendio estadístico, 1960* (1962).

13 P. G. Minneman, "Irrigation in Mexico" (unpublished manuscript, June 3, 1955).

14 P. G. Minneman, "Mexico's Agriculture" (American Embassy, México, D.F., Mar. 1, 1955, mimeographed).

15 Alfredo Navarrete, Jr., "Una hipótesis sobre el sistema económico de México," *El trimestre económico*, XVIII, January–March 1951.

16 Alfredo Navarrete, Jr. and Ifigenia M. de Navarrete, "La subocupación en las economías poco desarrolladas," *El trimestre económico*, XVIII, October–December 1951.

17 Adolfo Orive Alba, "Programa de irrigación del C. Presidente Miguel Alemán," *Ingenieria hidráulica en México*, I, January–March 1947.

---

[8] Several other significant multi-purpose schemes have since been initiated in the Mexican tropics. The somewhat smaller Tepalcatepec project (later merged into the Balsas scheme) was started in the lowlands of west-central Mexico shortly after the Papaloapan, and the vast Grijalva project to develop the river basin of the same name in the lowlands to the east of the Isthmus of Tehuantepec was begun in 1951. In addition, numerous minor works have been terminated or are in various stages of completion.

18 Adolfo Orive Alba, "Una tierra sedienta," in Mexico, Sec. Gober., *Seis años de actividad nacional* (1946).

19 Rockefeller Foundation, *Annual Report, 1955* (New York).

20 "Sinopsis del informe de labores de la secretaría de recursos hidraulicos (del 1°. de septiembre de 1960 al 31 de agosto de 1961)," *Ingeniería hidráulica en México*, XV, July–September 1961.

21 Adolf Sturmthal, "Economic Development, Income Distribution, and Capital Formation in Mexico," *The Journal of Political Economy*, LXIII, June 1955.

22 Frank Tannenbaum, *Mexico: The Struggle for Peace and Bread* (New York, 1951).

23 U.N., Dept. Soc. Aff., Pop. Div., *The Population of Central America (Including Mexico), 1950–1980* (New York, 1954).

24 U.N., Dept. Soc. Aff., Stat. Off., *Statistical Yearbook, 1961* (New York, 1961).

25 Emilio Uribe Romo, "La fuerza de trabajo de México: Un análisis de su estructura, sus características y su evolución," *Estadística*, XIII, June 1955.

26 C. C. Wallen, "Fluctuations and Variability in Mexican Rainfall," in G. F. White, ed., *The Future of Arid Lands* (Washington, 1956).

27 N. L. Whetten, *Rural Mexico* (Chicago, 1948).

28 Kathryn H. Wylie, "Food Consumption in Mexico," *Foreign Agriculture*, XIX, August 1955.

Chapter 3

THE PAPALOAPAN BASIN

The Papaloapan basin is situated directly west of the Isthmus of Tehuantepec. It is defined as embracing the catchment basins of the rivers that empty into the Gulf of Mexico through the Laguna de Alvarado: chiefly the Papaloapan and its tributaries, but also several lesser streams, notably the Río Blanco. The 17,800 square miles so delimited correspond roughly to the combined areas of Vermont and New Hampshire, and constitute 2.3 per cent of Mexico's land area. Politically, portions of three states—Veracruz, Oaxaca, and Puebla—are included.

PHYSICAL RESOURCES

Relief

Physiographically, the basin includes both highland and lowland segments. Of the two, the latter is significantly the larger; if the 100-meter contour line is taken as the boundary between plain and upland, roughly two-thirds of the basin is made up of highlands. The distribution of these regions appears in Maps 5 and 6.

The approximately 6,000 square miles that make up the area below the 100-meter contour are generally referred to as the lower basin.[1] It consists of a plain extending back from the Gulf of Mexico for about 45 or 50 miles, at which point the relief changes rather abruptly and becomes sharply ascending. While properly termed a plain, the coastal lowland is best described as varying between slightly undulating in most places to gently rolling as the elevation limits are approached. There are, however, substantial

---

[1] There is no universally accepted definition of the elevation limits of the lower basin. However, the 100-meter contour is most commonly employed by workers of the Papaloapan Commission for this purpose and is therefore used here.

31

MAP 5.—PAPALOAPAN BASIN: RELIEF

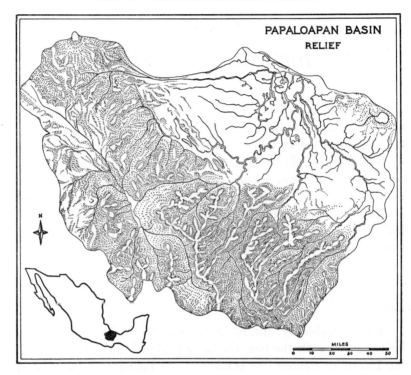

PAPALOAPAN BASIN
RELIEF

stretches of virtually level land along the margins of the principal streams, particularly as they near the Laguna de Alvarado, and in the area immediately behind this lake. Much of this level land has an elevation of less than 30 feet and a high water table; it includes numerous lakes and marshes, and has been especially subject to flooding or water intrusion during periods of heavy rain or high stream flow.

The high interior region southwest of the coastal plain is designated collectively as the upper basin, although it is actually composed of three clearly defined sub-areas. Immediately adjacent to the lower basin is the most important of these, the high and very rugged Sierra Madre Oriental, the mountain range that extends almost the length of eastern Mexico, separating the Gulf lowlands

MAP 6.—PAPALOAPAN BASIN: GENERALIZED ELEVATION*

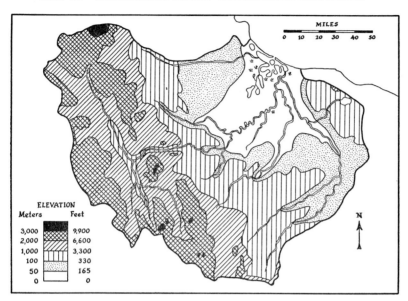

* Adapted from Mexico, Sec. Rec. Hid., Comisión del Papaloapan, *Atlas climatológico e hidrológico de la cuenca del Papaloapan* (1958), Plate 1.

from the interior plateaus. Within the basin the average elevation of the Sierra's spine is well over 6,000 feet. The southern part is dominated by an 11,000-foot peak, Mt. Zempoaltepec, the northern by Mt. Orizaba, which rises to some 18,700 feet.

The Sierra has been deeply dissected by the cutting action of numerous streams, so that it presents a series of steep, lateral escarpments as well as a main ridge. To the north of the Santo Domingo River, its eastern slope ascends rapidly from the floor of the lower basin and in places rises from 300 to over 6,500 feet in about 12 miles.[2] Southeast of the Santo Domingo, and particularly between the Tesechoacan and San Juan rivers, the gradient is relatively gentle. In this region a similar ascent requires an average of about 40 miles.

A few miles west of its crest the Sierra descends, again quite

[2] The basin's principal rivers and natural features are shown in Map 9 (p. 48).

abruptly, into the second sub-area of the upper basin, the Cañada Oaxaqueña-Poblana (Depression of Oaxaca and Puebla). This depression extends for some 70 miles at an average elevation of about 3,500 feet. The width of its floor varies between two and six miles. On the west the Cañada is bordered by the upper basin's third sub-area, the northeastern flank of the Sierra Mixteca, the principal range of southern Mexico. Within the basin this range does not reach the average height attained by the Sierra Madre, but it has been similarly dissected by stream erosion, and its slope is also composed of a series of rugged lateral escarpments.

The other upland region in the basin is completely separated from the upper basin, and lies on the northeastern fringe of the coastal lowlands. It consists of a portion of the Sierra de los Tuxtlas, a small, isolated range of volcanic origin that rises from the plains of southern Veracruz a few miles from the coast. Compared with the Sierra Madre this range is low, its highest peak being below 6,000 feet, the bulk of its slope falling within the basin below 3,000 feet.

Hydrology

The basin's river system has its origin in the highlands west of the main ridge of the Sierra Madre. There, numerous small rivulets flow into the Cañada and ultimately meet near its center to form the Santo Domingo, which drops through a precipitous cut in the Sierra Madre into the coastal plain. At the edge of the lowlands the Santo Domingo is joined in turn by the Valle Nacional and Tonto rivers, both of which have their headwaters in the eastern slope of the Sierra, and becomes the Papaloapan. This broad stream then meanders across the lower basin, is joined near the coast by the Tesechoacan and San Juan rivers (which rise in the southern portion of the Sierra's eastern slope), and finally empties into the Laguna de Alvarado. Several relatively minor streams which by definition are included within the Papaloapan basin also empty into this lake. The most important of these is the Río Blanco, which has its headwaters on the eastern slope of Mt. Orizaba.

The rate of fall of the geologically young rivers of the upper basin is generally rapid, so that they afford far greater potentialities for power generation than for navigation. The mature streams of the lowlands, on the other hand, have historically formed one of the principal means of communication in that area, but their slight grade and slow current have also rendered them particularly vulnerable to flooding. Owing to the marked seasonality of rainfall, some overflow occurs almost annually; and it is estimated that during the 50 years or so immediately preceding the institution of control measures under the Papaloapan Project, serious inundations occurred about once every four or five years.

The average annual discharge of the Papaloapan river system is about 43,000 million cubic meters, making it Mexico's second most important river in terms of flow. Because of the nature of much of the terrain traversed, this flow implies a substantial hydroelectric capability. In fact, the basin's potential generating capacity is placed at between .6 and .9 million kilowatts, about 25 per cent of the total capacity (hydro and thermal) currently installed in the country (14, p. 156; 8, p. 88). This potential is particularly significant in that it forms one of the largest reserves within economic transmission distance of the main centers of population and industry in the Central Mesa. These resources were largely untapped prior to the Papaloapan Project; in 1947 the installed capacity of hydroelectric plants in the basin—almost all of it dependent on the Río Blanco—amounted to only 50,000 kilowatts (1, p. 169).

Climate

The Papaloapan basin falls within the zone of the tropical marine climate type, and were it not for the modifying effect of relief, the climatic regime of the entire area could be so classified. As it is, the mountainous nature of the upper basin effectively restricts this warm and humid climate to the coastal plain, the Tuxtlas highlands, and the lower reaches of the eastern slope of the Sierra Madre. Most of the upper basin is cool and comparatively dry.

The effect of elevation upon temperature divides the basin into three relatively distinct, and popularly recognized, vertical cropping

Chart 4.—Altitude Limits of Vertical Crop Zones on the Slopes of Mt. Orizaba*

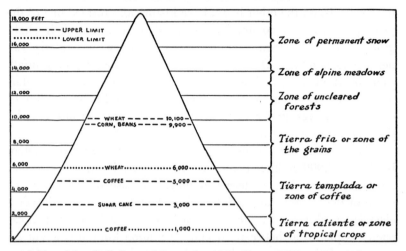

* Adapted from P. E. James, *A Geography of Man* (Boston, 1951), p. 404, which in turn was based on Karl Sapper, *Allgemeine Wirtschafts- und Verkehrsgeographie* (Berlin, 1930), pp. 66–67.

zones. (See Chart 4.) Of these the most important lies between sea level and about 2,100 feet, the hot and humid *tierra caliente*, the zone of the tropical crops. Something like 50 per cent of the basin falls in this zone, including, in addition to the coastal plain, most of the Tuxtlas highlands and the lower portion of the eastern slope of the Sierra Madre. Temperatures are high throughout the year, and, as the following data for Cosamaloapan (near the center of the lower basin) testify, exhibit very modest seasonal changes:[3]

Mean temperature	Mean temperature coolest month (January)	Mean temperature warmest month (May)
78.0° F.	71.6° F.	83.8° F.

Even the range between extremes is rather small; the lowest temperature recorded at Cosamaloapan is 48.2° F., while the highest is

[3] Temperature data in this and the following paragraph are for the period 1950–55, and are either taken directly or calculated from the detailed recordings published in Mexico, Sec. Rec. Hid., Comisión del Papaloapan, *Boletín hidrológico*, 1950 through 1955 (nos. 2–7, 1951–56).

106.7° F.—an extreme range of 58 degrees. With minimum temperatures well above freezing, the tierra caliente enjoys the year-long growing season required by such crops as bananas and sugar cane. It is this zone with which the Papaloapan Project is chiefly concerned.

Immediately above the tierra caliente and continuing to about 6,000 feet is the relatively mild *tierra templada*. Roughly 35 per cent of the basin's area lies in this zone. Its most notable components are the Cañada and the middle reaches of both slopes of the Sierra Madre. Temperatures here average about 10 degrees below those recorded in the tierra caliente, and again vary only slightly from one season to another. Killing frosts are almost unknown. At Villa Alta (in the southern portion of the Sierra Madre at 3,740 feet), for instance, the mean annual temperature is 68° F., and the lowest recorded reading is 34° F. Within the basin, the tierra templada is most commonly associated with the cultivation of coffee and similar crops requiring a mild, equable temperature.

Succeeding the tierra templada between the approximate limits of 6,000 and 10,100 feet is the *tierra fría*, the highest of the vertical strata in which agriculture is practiced. This zone includes most of the remaining 15 per cent of the basin's area, and is composed of all but the highest segments of the upper reaches of the Sierra Madre and the Sierra Mixteca. Although temperatures here average only about 10 degrees below those registered in the tierra templada, freezing is common during five or six months of the year. Thus the growing season is relatively short, and for this reason annual crops with short growing seasons, especially corn and small grains, are common.

The regional disparities in rainfall found in the basin are perhaps even more pronounced than those of temperature. Generally speaking, the areas east of the central massif of the Sierra Madre enjoy an abundance, in some parts even a superabundance, of rainfall, while those to the west suffer a serious deficit (Map 7). The highest precipitation is recorded in the eastern slope of the Sierra Madre, where it averages about 120 inches per year, and in places exceeds 160 inches. Rainfall is somewhat less plentiful in the coastal plain, but is nevertheless quite copious, ranging from about 60 to 80 inches. In sharp contrast, the western portions of the upper basin—the Sierra Mixteca, the Cañada, and the western slope of the Sierra Madre—receive only some 15 to 35 inches.

Rainfall in the basin is the result of two influences: convectional activity, associated with the northward migration of the intertropical convergence zone during the summer, and orographic lifting, chiefly in conjunction with the northeast trade wind, which prevails throughout much of the year. Of these, orographic lifting is the more important; not only is it the prime cause of precipitation, but it also accounts for the geographical distribution of rainfall (Chart 5). The trades, blowing over thousands of miles of tropical and semi-tropical ocean before reaching the basin, absorb increasing amounts of mois-

MAP 7.—PAPALOAPAN BASIN: AVERAGE ANNUAL RAINFALL
IN INCHES, 1926–55*

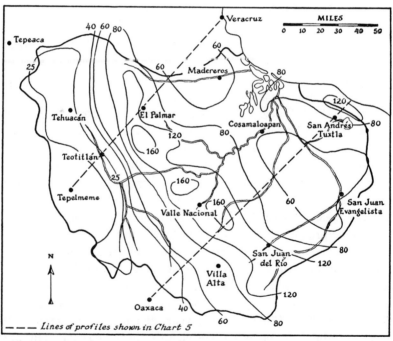

* Adapted from Mexico, Sec. Rec. Hid., Comisión del Papaloapan, *Atlas climatológico e hidrológico de la cuenca del Papaloapan* (1958), Plate 10.

CHART 5.—PROFILES ILLUSTRATING THE EFFECT OF TOPOGRAPHY
ON RAINFALL IN THE PAPALOAPAN BASIN*

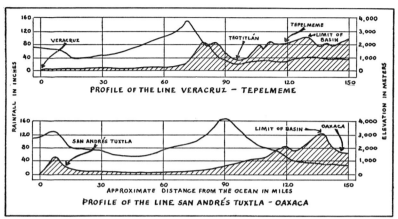

* Adapted from Mexico, Sec. Rec. Hid., Comisión del Papaloapan, *Atlas climatológico e hidrológico de la cuenca del Papaloapan* (1958), Plate 10.

ture as their temperature is raised by the equatorial sun and through contact with the warmer sea, and arrive at the basin's eastern margin heavily saturated. As they pass over the coastal plain and surrounding country, they are forced upward by the elevation of the land, become cooler, and release moisture. This precipitation attains its peak over the lower reaches of the Sierra Madre's eastern or windward slope, where forced ascension and cooling are greatest. On the leeward or western side of the Sierra, the air descends and becomes warmer, and consequently retains most of its moisture. The lee slope, the Cañada, and the Sierra Mixteca, therefore, lie in a "rain shadow" and are relatively dry.

Unlike temperature, the rainfall of the basin exhibits a marked seasonality. Throughout the area, there is a clearly defined rainy season extending from late May or early June through October (during which approximately 85 per cent of the yearly precipitation occurs), and a dry period between November and May. Within the wet season, as the graphs in Chart 6 indicate, there are two reasonably distinct rainfall maxima, one during June and July and the other in September. The June-July maximum is chiefly the result of particu-

CHART 6.—MONTHLY DISTRIBUTION OF RAINFALL AT SELECTED
STATIONS IN THE PAPALOAPAN BASIN, AVERAGE 1950–55*

(Inches; January–December)

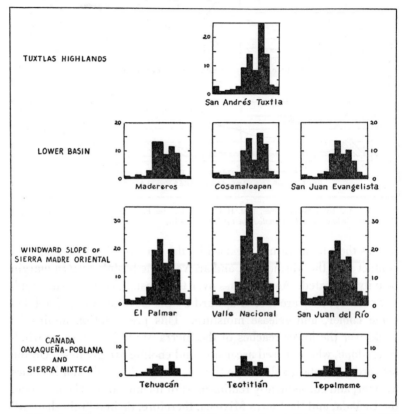

* Data from Mexico, Sec. Rec. Hid., Comisión del Papaloapan, *Boletín hidrológico,* 1950 through 1955 (nos. 2–7, 1951–56).

larly intense convectional activity as the sun approaches the zenith of its northward march, while the autumn peak is mainly orographic, the trade winds carrying their greatest moisture load when sea temperatures are highest following the period of summer heat.

The Caribbean hurricane, whose periodic visits to Mexico occur most frequently during September and October, also contributes to the autumn rainfall maximum. The basin lies within the limits of one of the three principal tracks followed by these violent cyclonic disturbances when they pass over the country, and is visited on an average of about once every five years (*3*, pp. 93–94, Map 6). These hurricanes are characterized by high winds and very heavy rainfall; in September 1944, for instance, because of an especially severe storm, Teotitlán received 21 inches of rainfall, only five inches less than the amount normally recorded during an entire year (*15*, part 1, p. 22). Because of the high intensity of the rainfall they bring, hurricanes have been the prime cause of flooding in the lower basin.

The combined effects of geographical distribution and seasonality of rainfall on the basin's agricultural potentials are illustrated in Map 8. This map shows the number of months in which the vari-

MAP 8.—PAPALOAPAN BASIN: NUMBER OF MONTHS IN WHICH UTILIZABLE RAINFALL EXCEEDS 24 MILLIMETERS WITH 80 PER CENT PROBABILITY*

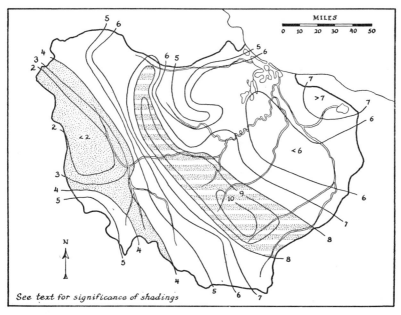

* Adapted from Mexico, Sec. Rec. Hid., Comisión del Papaloapan, *Atlas climatológico e hidrológico de la cuenca del Papaloapan* (1958), Plate 20.

ous portions of the area can expect to receive at least 24 millimeters (.95 inch) of utilizable rainfall with 80 per cent probability—that is, during four out of every five years. In preparing the map, utilizable rainfall (i.e., that portion of total rainfall which is not lost through surface runoff or evaporation, but which finds its way into the root zone) was estimated at 75 per cent of the volume of all rains exceeding 5 millimeters. The significance of 24 millimeters of utilizable rainfall is that it represents the estimated monthly moisture requirement of corn, in acreage by far the most important crop of the basin and one grown throughout all three of the vertical temperature zones (6, pp. 2–6).

On the basis of the data in this map, the basin may be thought of as including three general (and vaguely defined and delimited) rainfall zones. In the first zone, the moisture supply is sufficient for two crops of corn—or of other annuals with more or less the same moisture requirements and growing period (about four months)—to be harvested yearly with an 80 per cent probability of success. In the second, a single harvest can be taken during the rainy season, but irrigation is required for a second crop. In the third, irrigation is necessary for the reasonably secure production of even one crop. These zones are indicated in the map by striped shading, the absence of shading, and solid shading, respectively.

In terms of the area encompassed, the second zone—where one unirrigated crop is feasible annually—is the most important; it includes the lower basin, the Tuxtlas highlands, the upper reaches of both slopes of the Sierra Madre, and a small segment of the Sierra Mixteca. Taken together, these regions make up over two-thirds of the basin's surface. Agriculture in this zone is marked by a distinct seasonality of production. Annual crops planted at the onset of the rainy period are the general rule, although some perennials requiring a well-defined, even though short, dry season are also widespread, notably sugar cane in the coastal plain and coffee in the uplands. Only in the wetter sections of the zone, the Tuxtlas highlands and the western fringe of the lower basin, are dry-season crops commonly attempted.

The lower portion of the Sierra's windward slope is roughly coterminous with the zone in which rainfall is generally adequate for the production of two successive corn crops during the year. Since this area also falls within the tierra caliente, agriculture is practicable throughout the year. Accordingly, both annual and perennial crops thrive here. However, because inclined terrain and extremely heavy rainfall combine to pose a serious threat to soil stability, the region is more suited to such perennial tree crops as bananas, cocoa, and rubber than to the various cultivated tropical annuals.

The rain-shadow portion of the western upper basin corresponds to the third zone, in which a modest and exceedingly variable rainfall regime essentially precludes the establishment of a prosperous agricultural economy except under irrigation. Unfortunately, the rugged nature of the region's topography restricts the feasibility of all but very minor irrigation works to the floor of the Cañada. As a result, most of the area is almost wholly unsuited to a stable agricultural system based on the crops and rudimentary techniques currently employed, and those peasants who attempt to eke a living from an occasional harvest are predestined to a life of poverty.

Vegetation

Owing to the wide regional disparities in rainfall and temperature, the vegetation of the basin is widely diversified. Savanna with scattered trees and open forests intermixed with savanna form the dominant patterns of natural cover in the hot and seasonally watered coastal plain. As the elevation limits of the plain are approached (and rainfall becomes heavier and the dry season less pronounced), these patterns give way to a pattern of luxuriant evergreen tropical forests which continues through the Tuxtlas highlands and the lower portion of the Sierra Madre's windward slope. In the higher and cooler reaches of the Sierra, this tropical cover is succeeded in turn by dense and relatively homogeneous stands of deciduous hardwoods and of conifers. These forests continue down the western slope of the Sierra, but as the amount of rainfall declines they become increasingly more open and their growth becomes less vigorous. Finally, in the vicinity of the Cañada, they give way altogether to very spotty xerophytic cover, which characterizes the semi-arid rain shadow of the western upper basin.

The forests of the basin cover about a third of its area and are one of its most valuable resources. Especially noteworthy with respect to their economic potentials are the extensive hardwood and coniferous stands found in the eastern highlands of the Sierra Madre. It is estimated that about 300,000 hectares of pure coniferous forest and roughly an equal area of hardwoods can be found in the southern half of this region alone (map accompanying *16*). Though the more heterogeneous tropical forests of the lower elevations are on the whole of less potential value, they contain numerous marketable species, including mahogany, white mahogany, and cedar.

Prior to the Papaloapan Project, transportation deficiencies precluded all but a modest degree of commercial exploitation of these forests. Only 25 small mills, with a combined daily output of less than 10,000 board-feet, were in operation in 1947, most of them in the eastern portion of the lower basin. This is not to imply that all of the basin's forests were then essentially in a virgin state. Shifting cultivation in the tropical sections had reduced many stands to secondary growth, and throughout many of the more populated areas indiscriminate cutting for firewood had taken a heavy toll. Particularly in the western parts of the Sierra Madre and in the Sierra Mixteca, where cover was none too dense to begin with, deforestation had proceeded at an alarming rate. Yet, in much of the wooded area, especially in the Sierra Madre's eastern slope, vast stands remained virtually unmolested (*1*, pp. 10–12).

Soils

The soil resources of the basin remain largely an unknown quantity. It is no credit to the Papaloapan Commission that after 16 years it has yet to conduct a soil reconnaissance of the region or systematically investigate the capabilities of the various soil types. About all that has been assembled so far are a few preliminary studies of minor areas in which the Commission has had a particular interest and one or two general surveys of a highly superficial nature. These suffice for an introduction; but on more than one occasion the absence of more thorough information has caused the Commission to make expensive mistakes.

As in tropical and semi-tropical regions the world over, the dominant type of soil found in the basin is the laterite (5). These soils are formed under conditions of abundant rainfall and high temperatures, and bear all the marks of intense weathering and rapid organic decaying. The process of laterization is essentially one of extreme weathering: the bases and silica are leached out of the soil's parent material, leaving it rich only in aluminum and iron. These soils accordingly are characterized by a reddish color and by a deficiency of available plant nutrients. Excessive decaying and leaching, moreover, have resulted in a low percentage of organic matter, which is confined to a thin layer near the surface. Though their texture is invariably heavy, the laterites are usually quite pervious to water because of their low silica content, and in most instances can be worked almost immediately after even the heaviest rains (9, pp. 345–47).

If a substantial variability in the productiveness of these soils has been noted within the basin, their fertility level seems to be unimpressive. In the absence of precautionary measures, virgin plots tend to becomes quickly exhausted when cleared and cultivated; under the present primitive farming techniques practiced in the area, a given clearing is commonly abandoned and returned to natural cover after only one or two years of cropping. Laterites are found throughout all but the drier sections of the basin, and are particularly common in the plains between the rivers of the lower basin and in the lower reaches of the southern half of the Sierra Madre's windward slope.

Less widely distributed than the laterites, but at present of considerably greater economic importance, are the two other main soil types of the basin: the recent alluviums and the soils of volcanic origin. Of these, the alluvial soils are the more important since they enjoy a comparatively wide distribution along the margins of the numerous rivers that cross the lower basin. Formed of materials continually being deposited during times of high stream flow, they are generally deep, rich, and highly productive. The volcanic soils are also quite fertile, but appear to be somewhat more limited in their incidence. They are found chiefly around the bases and slopes of the basin's two extinct volcanic complexes, Mt. Orizaba and the Tuxtlas highlands. However, small outcroppings seem to exist throughout the coastal lowlands.

Minerals

The sub-soil resources of the basin, though also little understood, are considered to be substantial. Preliminary investigations have revealed that a wide variety of minerals awaits extraction, particularly in the upper basin. Gold and silver have been mined in this region since at least the time of the Conquest; and, of the more important industrial metals, lead, copper, mercury, zinc, and uranium are known to exist in considerable quantities. In the lower basin promising deposits of natural gas, petroleum, and sulphur have been uncovered during the past decade; but, as is the case generally for the mineral resources of the basin, the extent of these finds has yet to be fully assessed (*17*, pp. 24–25; *1*, pp. 107–9; *14*, pp. 123–24).

As with virtually all of the basin's other natural resources, this sub-soil wealth was little exploited prior to the Papaloapan Project. Even the existence of many of the deposits was then unknown, and primitive transport facilities essentially precluded extraction of all but minerals with a very high unit value (i.e., gold and silver). In 1947 the total value of the yearly output of the basin's mines, most of them situated in the Sierra Madre to the north and east of the city of Oaxaca, was estimated at only 5 million pesos ($1 million at the rate of exchange then prevailing) (*1*, pp. 108, 111).

HUMAN RESOURCES[4]

Population Distribution

The Papaloapan basin contains about 4.5 per cent of Mexico's population—in 1950, some 1,130,000 people. As it occupies 2.3 per cent of the country's area, its mean population density is approximately double the national average. Nevertheless, the basin as a whole cannot be considered heavily populated, especially when compared with the Central Mesa; its mean density of 64 persons per square mile in 1950 amounted only to about half the average of 117 for the ten states and Federal District roughly coinciding with that region (*10*, p. 4). But such comparisons are of little value in describing the density of population, for the basin contains stretches of virtually unoccupied land and also some of the most heavily populated sections of Mexico. A much clearer picture may be obtained from Map 9, which shows all the communities having 1,000 or more inhabitants in 1950. These centers together contain about half the people in the basin, and their locations are indicative of the distribution of the entire population.

The heaviest concentration is found in the northwestern corner of the upper basin. Here, in a region (the approximate southern boundary of which is shown in Map 9 by a dotted line) making up 10 per cent of the total area, live some 31 per cent of the people, giving it an average density approaching 200 per square mile. Unlike the rest of the basin, this region is semi-urban, and includes the area's four largest cities. In 1950, the towns of Orizaba, Córdoba, Tehuacán, and Ciudad Mendoza contained over a third of the region's 350,-000 people. The concentration here is to be explained largely in terms of strategic location. The area straddles one of the two traditional routes connecting the port of Veracruz with the Central Mesa, and has historically participated more actively in Mexico's economic life than any other section of the basin.

About 35 per cent of the population (some 400,000 people in 1950) live in the remainder of the upper basin. The inhabitants of this vast hinterland are for the most part found in the higher and cooler reaches of the Sierra Madre, particularly in the area immediately south of the semi-urban portion, around Huautla, and east of the city of Oaxaca. In these areas the mean density is about 60 persons per square mile. Elsewhere the density is much lower; in the

[4] Unless otherwise noted, the statistics in the remainder of this chapter have been calculated from data in the 1950 Census of Population as reported in *11, 12,* and *13.* For a discussion of the census data for the Papaloapan basin employed in this study, including the data from the 1950 Census of Agriculture utilized in Chapter 4, see the Appendix, p. 159.

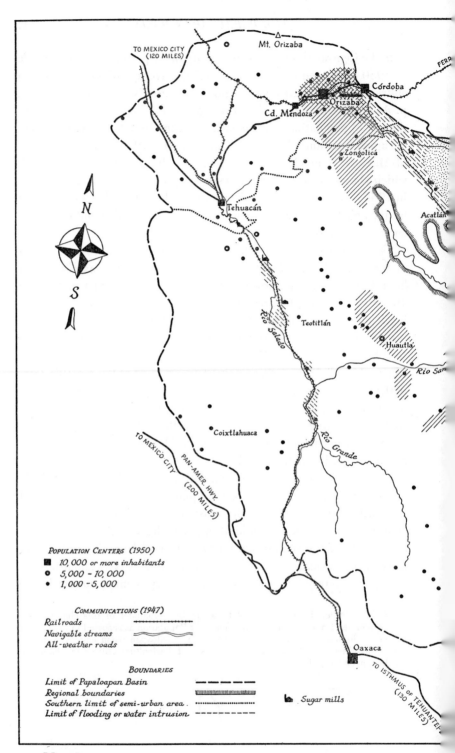

TO MEXICO CITY
(120 MILES)

Mt. Orizaba

FERR

Córdoba

Cd. Mendoza

Orizaba

Zongolica

Acatlán

N

S

Tehuacán

Río Saludo

Teotitlán

Huautla

Río San

Coixtlahuaca

Río Grande

TO MEXICO CITY

PAN-AMER. HWY
(200 MILES)

POPULATION CENTERS (1950)
◼ 10,000 or more inhabitants
◉ 5,000 – 10,000
• 1,000 – 5,000

COMMUNICATIONS (1947)
Railroads
Navigable streams
All-weather roads

BOUNDARIES
Limit of Papaloapan Basin
Regional boundaries
Southern limit of semi-urban area
Limit of flooding or water intrusion

Sugar mills

Oaxaca

TO ISTHMUS OF TEHUANTE-
(130 MILES)

MAP 9

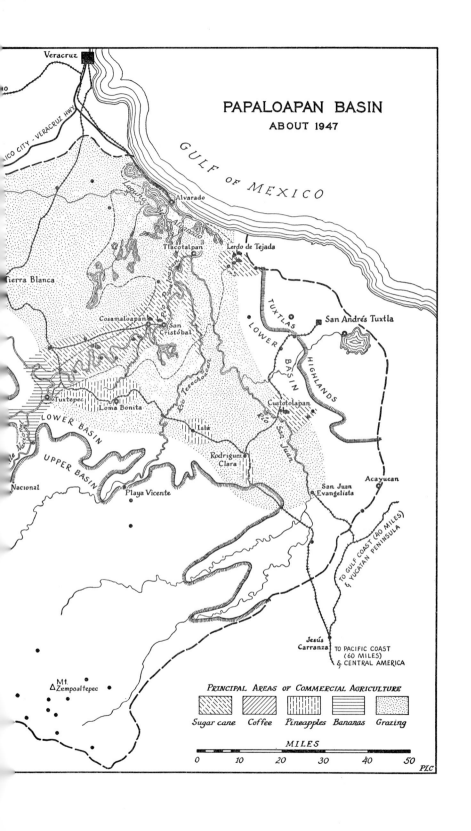

PAPALOAPAN BASIN
ABOUT 1947

Veracruz

MEXICO CITY - VERACRUZ HWY.

GULF OF MEXICO

Laguna de Alvarado

Alvarado

Tlacotalpan

Lerdo de Tejada

Tierra Blanca

Río Papaloapan

TUXTLAS

San Andrés Tuxtla

Cosamaloapan

San Cristóbal

LOWER BASIN

HIGHLANDS

Río Tesechoacán

Tuxtepec

Loma Bonita

Cuatotolapan

LOWER BASIN

Isla

Río San Juan

Valle Nacional

UPPER BASIN

Rodríguez Clara

Acayucan

Nacional

Playa Vicente

San Juan Evangelista

TO GULF COAST (40 MILES) & YUCATAN PENINSULA

Jesús Carranza   TO PACIFIC COAST
(60 MILES)
& CENTRAL AMERICA

Mt. Δ Zempoaltepec

PRINCIPAL AREAS OF COMMERCIAL AGRICULTURE

Sugar cane   Coffee   Pineapples   Bananas   Grazing

MILES

0   10   20   30   40   50

PLC

Sierra Mixteca, for instance, it averages about 30 persons per square mile, and in the windward slope area to the southeast of Valle Nacional it amounts to only about 10 per square mile.

The lower basin and the Tuxtlas highlands, with a combined population in 1950 of roughly 380,000, contain the remaining 34 per cent of the people. Here the population is concentrated along the margins of the Papaloapan, the Tesechoacan, and the lower Blanco rivers (about 100 persons per square mile), in and around the periphery of the Tuxtlas highlands (roughly 75 per square mile), and, to a lesser degree, along the rail lines. In the plains between the rivers, on the other hand, the average density ranges between but 5 and 15 per square mile, if the sections served by railroad are excluded from consideration. This distribution mirrors the influence of soil quality on human settlement in the humid tropics: the alluvial soils of the river margins and the volcanic soils of the Tuxtlas area enjoy a productivity far greater than that of the lateritic soils found in the interfluvial plains. But a contributing factor of considerable importance has been the availability of communications. Prior to the first decade of the present century, the rivers of the lower basin represented the only means by which people and produce could be moved with any degree of ease. The significance of communications is attested to by the number of communities that have since sprung up along the railroads in the non-riparian sections; typically, the soils in these areas are no more fertile than in the surrounding sparsely settled regions.

The population of the basin is predominantly rural, with most of the people living in small villages and depending directly on agriculture for their livelihood. According to the 1950 Census, which classified as "rural" all persons residing in communities having less than 2,500 inhabitants, 70 per cent of the population is rural. This figure, however, understates the rural nature of the area. Instead of living on the land, the Mexican peasant typically has his home in a small village and walks daily to and from his plot of land. For this reason, population centers generally do not take on a truly urban character until they have 5,000 or 10,000 inhabitants (*19*, p. 35). If these be accepted as more valid criteria, then only 14 to 21 per cent of the population can be considered as living in urban centers. Of this number, over two-thirds reside in the four cities of the semi-urban region. The remainder live in some 15 towns of modest size, the largest of which, San Andrés Tuxtla, boasted a population of only 15,000 in 1950.

Cultural Configuration

Culturally, the people of the basin present a heterogeneity probably unequaled in any other section of Mexico. Included are persons separated by literally centuries of ethnographical development, ranging from Indians whose way of living has changed only moderately since pre-Cortesian times to people with a modern culture predominantly European in orgin. This variation is a reflection of the region's geographical diversity and its effect on communications. In the portions where geography has facilitated or at least not hindered the spread of communications, European influences typically have taken a firm hold; where the lay of the land is inhospitable, on the other hand, indigenous cultural traits remain strongly entrenched.

Probably the best available indicator of the extent to which European as opposed to predominantly indigenous ways of life prevail in the various sections of the basin, and of the extent to which the people participate in the civilization of modern Mexico, is the proportion of the population speaking Spanish rather than Indian tongues. As Table 1 shows, this proportion varies significantly between the several sections.[5] Taken as a whole, the people of the semi-urban area, 92 per cent of whom habitually speak Spanish, are the most Europeanized in the basin. Located along one of the main routes between Mexico City and Veracruz, and since 1873 traversed by the principal rail line connecting these points, this region has traditionally shared in the developing national socio-cultural life. Its four major towns

[5] The data given in Table 1 probably overstate somewhat the predominance of Spanish-speaking people by exaggerating the number of true bilinguals. Investigations of specific portions of the basin indicate that many, if not most, of the "bilinguals" speak and understand only a few words of Spanish. Something of a social stigma is attached to not being able to speak Spanish, and it is only natural that people with a mere smattering of that language should desire to be recorded as bilingual. It is therefore likely that a majority of the people reported as bilingual are actually fluent only in an indigenous tongue, and are better grouped with the Indian-speaking monolinguals.

TABLE 1.—PAPALOAPAN BASIN: PERSONS FIVE YEARS OF AGE OR
OLDER CLASSIFIED ACCORDING TO LANGUAGE SPOKEN, BY REGION,
1950*

| | | | | | Indian | | | | | | Total | |
| | Spanish | | Exclusively | | With Spanish | | Total | | (cols. 1 and 4) | |
Region	Number	%	Number	%	Number	%	Number	%	Number	%
Lower basin and										
Tuxtlas area	273,155	85	19,082	6	27,358	9	46,440	15	319,595	100
Upper basin:										
Semi-urban portion ..	275,810	92	7,465	2	17,553	6	25,018	8	300,828	100
Hinterland	95,212	28	115,300	34	130,087	38	245,387	72	340,599	100
Total basin	644,177	67	141,847	15	174,998	18	316,845	33	961,022	100

* Calculated from Mexico, Sec. Econ., Dir. Gen. Estad., Séptimo   de Puebla (1953); and ibid., Estado de Veracruz (1953).
censo general de población. Estado de Oaxaca (1953); ibid., Estado

are modern, semi-industrial centers on a par with all but the largest cities of the country.

European influences also prevail in the lower basin and in the Tuxtlas highlands, where about 85 per cent of the people are Spanish speaking. Here the extensive network of navigable streams has historically afforded the heavily populated riparian sections a means of access to the rest of the country. Then too, several railroads have served the area since the early part of the present century, and these have acted to increase the social mobility of the population and to encourage progress in general.

In the hinterland of the upper basin the process of acculturation has proceeded very slowly. Here live Indians who for centuries have existed on the fringe of civilization and whose traditional way of life has changed only superficially since the Conquest; less than 30 per cent of them characteristically speak Spanish.[6] Prior to the Papaloapan Project this region was almost completely isolated from the rest of Mexico, its rugged terrain having precluded all but the most primitive means of communication. The single exception was a narrow-gauge rail line passing through the Cañada.

The extreme cultural isolation of the inhabitants of the upper basin's interior is illustrated by the fact that outside of the Yucatan Peninsula there is no other section in Mexico of equivalent size and population with such a high proportion of Indian-speaking people (7, map facing p. 116). No less than nine mutually unintelligible indigenous languages survive in the area. Each corresponds to a more or less internally sufficient group (or, perhaps more descriptively, "tribe") having its own semi-communal economy, social order, dress, customs, and, after generations of inbreeding, a degree of ethnic identity. Primarily because of the language barrier, these groups have tended to regard even neighboring peoples as "foreigners," and exhibit a primitive provincialism suspicious of and unreceptive to

---

[6] Unlike the people of the rest of the basin and of Mexico as a whole who are chiefly mestizo, the inhabitants of the upper basin's interior are for the most part of pure Indian stock, because Spanish attempts to establish communities in the area during the sixteenth century met with failure. For detailed descriptions of some of the indigenous groups of the area and their way of life, see *2, 4,* and *17.*

new ideas. So backward are they, in fact, that among at least two of the groups, the Chinantecs and the Mazatecs, the pre-Cortesian calendar (which divides the year into 18 months of 20 days) is still in use, though only in connection with the initiation of various agricultural activities (*18*). Needless to say, economic growth in the area has been slight, and in most sections the economy is essentially at the subsistence level.

CITATIONS

1 José Attolini, *Economía de la cuenca del Papaloapan: Bosques, fauna, pesca, ganadería e industria* (México, D.F., 1950).

2 R. L. Beals, *Ethnology of the Western Mixe* (Univ. of Calif. Publications in American Archaeology and Ethnology, vol. 42, no. 1, 1945).

3 Aurelio Benassini and Andrés García Quintero, "Recursos hidráulicos de la república mexicana," *Ingenieria hidráulica en México*, IX, October–December 1955.

4 Bernard Bevan, *The Chinantec* (Instituto Panamericano de Geografía e Historia, México, D.F., 1938).

5 Jacques Butterlin, "Reconocimiento pedológico de la cuenca del Papaloapan (Informe preliminar)" (Comisión del Papaloapan, June 1956, unpublished).

6 Estudios y Proyectos, A. C., *Estudio preliminar de la precipitación versus requerimientos de los cultivos* (2d ed., México, D.F., 1955).

7 Armando González Santos, *La Agricultura: Estructura y utilización de los recursos* (México, D.F., and Buenos Aires, 1957).

8 "Hydro-electric Resources in Latin America: Their Measurement and Utilization," *Economic Bulletin for Latin America*, VII, February 1962.

9 T. L. Lyon, H. O. Buckman, and N. C. Brady, *The Nature and Properties of Soils* (5th ed., New York, 1952).

10 Mexico, Sec. Econ., Dir. Gen. Estad., *México en cifras, 1952*.

11 Mexico, Sec. Econ., Dir. Gen. Estad., *Septimo censo general de población. Estado de Oaxaca* (1953).

12 Mexico, Sec. Econ., Dir. Gen. Estad., *Septimo censo general de población. Estado de Puebla* (1953).

13 Mexico, Sec. Econ., Dir. Gen. Estad., *Septimo censo general de población. Estado de Veracruz* (1953).

14 Mexico, Sec. Rec. Hid., Comisión del Papaloapan, *Economía del Papaloapan: Evaluación de las inversiones y sus efectos* (1958).

15 J. S. Noriega, "Control del río Papaloapan: Preparación del plan de estudios definitivos y programa de construcción de las obras," *Ingenieria hidráulica en México*, I, April–June 1947 (part 1) ; and *ibid.*, I, July–September 1947 (part 2).

16 J. L. Tamayo, "El transporte ferrocarrilero en la cuenca del Papaloapan" (Comisión del Papaloapan, November 1954, unpublished).

17 Alfonso Villa Rojas, *Los Mazatecos y el problema indigena de la cuenca del Papaloapan* (Memorias del Instituto Nacional Indigenista, vol. VII, México, D. F., 1955).

18 R. J. Weitlaner and Irmgard Weitlaner, "The Mazatec Calendar," *American Antiquity*, XI, January 1946.

19 N. L. Whetten, *Rural Mexico* (Chicago, 1948).

Chapter 4

THE AGRICULTURAL ECONOMY
OF THE BASIN

The economy of the Papaloapan basin is overwhelmingly agricultural. In 1950, the latest year for which census data are available, fully 70 per cent of its labor force depended directly on farming or associated pursuits for a livelihood (Table 2). Only in the upper basin's semi-urban area were more than a quarter of the gainfully employed occupied in non-agricultural jobs, and even there farming was the most important source of employment. Yet the pre-eminent role of agriculture is even greater than these figures suggest. A substantial segment of non-farm employment arises either in the processing and marketing of agricultural commodities or in providing goods and services to the agrarian population.

Non-agricultural endeavors play a truly significant part only in the economy of the semi-urban portion. There a modest industrial complex has developed in and around Orizaba, Córdoba, and Ciudad

TABLE 2.—PAPALOAPAN BASIN: ECONOMICALLY ACTIVE PERSONS CLASSIFIED ACCORDING TO OCCUPATION, BY REGION, 1950*

Region	Economically active persons	Per cent occupied		
		Agriculture[a]	Industry	Other[b]
Lower basin and Tuxtlas area.....	118,952	77	7	16
Upper basin:				
Semi-urban portion	119,841	51	22	27
Hinterland	129,353	83	10	7
Total basin	368,146	70	13	17

* Calculated from Mexico, Sec. Econ., Dir. Gen. Estad., *Septimo censo general de población. Estado de Oaxaca* (1953); *ibid., Estado de Puebla* (1953); and *ibid., Estado de Veracruz* (1953). Economically active persons defined as those with remunerative employment at time of census, plus those who had been unemployed for less than 12 weeks.
[a] Includes forestry, hunting, and fishing.
[b] Commerce, services, transportation, and miscellaneous.

56

Mendoza, based on textile manufacturing, beer making, and sugar milling. Elsewhere, the contribution of non-farm activities to primary employment is slight. Such industry as is found in the interior of the upper basin is of the handicraft, or "cottage," variety, and mainly consists of the making of panama hats, while in the lower basin the majority of the small group of industrial workers are engaged in processing sugar, the area's chief commercial crop (*4*, pp. 128–38).[1]

As in most of the world's underdeveloped areas, the almost total absence of industries and the consequent dependence on agriculture means widespread economic backwardness; in tropical Mexico it is also indicative of an agriculture whose potentials have been only superficially tapped. Insofar as land under exploitation is concerned, the 1950 Census reported a mere 10 per cent of the basin's territory as planted to either field or tree crops, and only 25 per cent as used for grazing.[2] Moreover, of the fraction utilized, only a minor segment is exploited on a commercial basis. Less than a quarter of the area cultivated in 1949/50 was planted to crops destined for the market, while the remainder was devoted to a primitive form of subsistence farming.[3]

ECONOMIC IMPEDIMENTS TO DEVELOPMENT

Transportation

Apart from considerations growing out of physical environment and the cultural make-up of the population, one factor has gone far toward shaping the backward character of the basin's agricultural economy: isolation. Despite the proximity of the region to the con-

---

[1] The handicraft industry of the upper basin is most important in the semi-arid Sierra Mixteca, particularly in the vicinity of Coixtlahuaca, and occupies members of about 5,000 families (*4*, pp. 143–44).

[2] Unless otherwise noted, the statistics in this chapter have been calculated from data in the 1950 Census of Agriculture as reported in *14, 15*, and *17*.

[3] This breakdown is, of course, a crude one. It is impossible to clearly divide the crops of the basin into commercial and subsistence types, since few if any enter wholly into commercial channels. Nor are there any trustworthy data, save for one or two crops, to indicate the portions that find their way into the market. It is known, however, that among the major crops, most of the production of sugar cane, coffee, pineapples, bananas, and tobacco (which together occupied 22 per cent of the harvested area in 1949/50) is destined for the market, while the greater part of the production of most other crops is consumed on the farm.

suming centers of the Central Mesa, its transport system was so inadequate until the Papaloapan Project's inception in 1947 that most of
the territory was cut off physically from the national market economy.

In 1947 less than a quarter of the area lay within five miles of
reasonably satisfactory transport facilities, with only the semi-urban
portion enjoying comparatively acceptable service. Elsewhere, the
arterial network, consisting of a few ill-equipped and ill-maintained
railroads and of small, shallow-draft launches operating in the navigable portions of the river system, was woefully deficient. In addition, satisfactory feeder facilities were almost totally absent. Aside
from a few miles of ungraded dirt road, the secondary transport
routes consisted of a primitive system of paths and trails.

The location of railways, navigable streams, and principal roads
as of about 1947 are shown on Map 9. While far from being adequately served, the coastal plain, with a fairly widespread network of
railroads and navigable rivers, enjoyed vastly better facilities than
the highlands. Outside of the semi-urban section, the upper basin was
entirely devoid of modern means of transportation, save for one narrow-gauge railroad passing through the Cañada. The heavily populated highlands of the Sierra Madre were accessible only by trail, and
thus were almost wholly cut off from the national economy.

Of the several rail lines which serve the basin, and which from the
latter part of the nineteenth century until the advent of the Papaloapan Project formed the principal means of access to outside markets,
only one, the Ferrocarril Mexicano, could be regarded as providing
reasonably adequate service at the time the project was started.[4] Poor
maintenance and a chronic shortage of rolling stock severely restricted the benefits accruing to the territories served by other lines.
The condition of the Córdoba–Jesús Carranza trunk, for instance,

---

[4] This line, completed in 1873, connects the port of Veracruz with Mexico City and
the Central Mesa via the traditional trade route through Córdoba and Orizaba.
Although it runs through the northwestern corner of the basin for only about 50
miles, it embodied the first means of rapid access to the consuming centers of the
Central Mesa, and has played a crucial part in encouraging the development of the
entire region's economy. Only after its construction did industry take hold in the
semi-urban area, or commercial agriculture become established in the basin as a
whole.

was described as "poor," and even in favorable circumstances trains were invariably four to five hours late. The state of the shorter lines was even more wretched, rarely permitting trains to exceed 15 miles per hour. The Tierra Blanca–Veracruz roadbed was in such ill repair that the bulk of traffic between these points had to be routed through Córdoba, and trains on the San Cristóbal spur required at least four hours to cover its 30 miles (24; 9, pp. 83, 185; 6, p. 27).

Until the beginning of the twentieth century, commercial transportation outside of the semi-urban section was limited to the various navigable rivers, and hence to the broad streams of the lower basin. To reach outside markets, the products of the lowlands, then chiefly cotton and tobacco, were moved downstream to Alvarado and then up the coast by lighter to Veracruz. During these years the river system seems to have been in comparatively good condition, and by the late 1800's commercial traffic appears to have been appreciable. In the following half-century, however, it was sharply curtailed. Not only did extension of the rail network into the lowlands offer many areas a more attractive alternative; the physical condition of the rivers deteriorated drastically.[5]

So bad had things become by the mid-1940's that, save for a few short runs between otherwise isolated producing areas and the railroads, commercial water service had all but ceased. The principal streams within a radius of about 40 miles of Alvarado still had relatively deep channels, but nearer the Sierra a dramatic upturn in the siltation rate (which also caused a rise in the frequency and severity of flooding) had rendered their beds quite shallow. These deposits had become so large that the system was generally navigable to the extent shown in Map 9 only by craft drawing less than 20 inches, and then only during the rainy season. In the dry season, and particularly during the March–May period, low flow effectively restricted all commercial movement to the lower half of the system (9, pp. 76–80).

Primarily because the poor condition of the stream beds permits only craft of shallow draft and low tonnage to be employed, river transportation in the lower basin continues to be so inefficient that,

---

[5] The main rail system of the lower basin was constructed between 1890 and 1907.

contrary to the general rule, transport by water is usually more expensive than by rail or by road. The motor launches used are of a variety of sizes, but few have a cargo capacity in excess of 10 tons. They are generally very old and slow, being capable of averaging only three or four miles per hour and of attaining a maximum speed of about five. The barges are also quite small, and the largest, with capacities up to 100 tons, are used exclusively in the lower reaches. Efficiency of service is further reduced by the lack of adequate dock facilities except at Alvarado and the sugar mill at San Cristóbal. Elsewhere, all cargoes are loaded and unloaded by hand, a process that is both slow and costly, and also highly conducive to losses (9, p. 80; 2, p. 4).

By 1947 the national highway network, begun in 1924, had made little progress in the basin, and affected only the economy of the semi-urban region, the sole area that previously could be considered as enjoying adequate arterial facilities. The highway traversing this area is one of two that connect the Central Mesa with Veracruz. By 1935 it had been constructed as far east as Tehuacán, and several years later it was extended to Córdoba. The Córdoba–Veracruz section was not completed as an all-weather road until almost a decade later. Although the Puebla–Oaxaca–Tehuantepec portion of the Pan-American highway, completed in the early 1940's, lay but a few miles from the southwestern periphery of much of the upper basin, it had little effect on the inhabitants of that area owing to a complete absence of feeder roads.

With the exception of a "very mediocre" road between Alvarado and Veracruz, no other roads were linked to the national highway system. But in the lowlands a few ungraded dirt roads joined nearby villages with the railroads. These roads were virtually useless for motor vehicles, however, being passable only during the dry season and then with difficulty (9, p. 82).

Narrow trails best suited to ox-carts, pack trains, or human carriers formed the principal secondary transport routes in both the upper and lower basins. In the lowlands these trails typically paralleled the streams and railroads or radiated from them for generally no more than five or six miles. Given the time, difficulty, and expense required to move goods over such a rudimentary feeder system, it followed that most of the basin was cut off from the national market economy, and that most commercial production was restricted to narrow bands adjacent to the principal transport facilities. Indeed, so isolated was the region around Valle Nacional before the Papaloapan Project (despite its location on a navigable stream) that during the latter part of the Díaz dictatorship (1876–1910) it harbored a vicious system of virtual slave labor, and during the Revolution of 1910 was regarded as an excellent depository for political prisoners (*26*, pp. 67–108; *10*, p. 33).

Credit and Marketing

The confining of most marketable output to strips along the few trade routes has not, however, been the only obstacle to agricultural progress posed by inadequate transport facilities. Poor communications have also tended to fragmentize the market into a multitude of tiny, local divisions, and to perpetuate a deeply rooted system of advance purchase of crops. Under this system, essentially a carry-over of that used by the *tienda de raya* (plantation store) of the pre-Revolutionary hacienda, the processor or rural trader finances the operations of needy peasants in exchange for the exclusive privilege of buying their excess output. Almost the sole means by which the small grower in the less accessible portions of Mexico has traditionally been able to produce and market a surplus, the system enabled a restricted group of local traders and processors to gain control of most of the basin's commercial output.

There are numerous variations, but the advance-purchase system generally operates as follows. Sometime after his crop has been planted, the peasant approaches the trader, customarily the only person in his community with surplus funds or commercial connections, for a loan to help cover the costs of cultivating and harvesting. If granted, the loan carries no interest charge, but requires as a basic condition that the entire harvest be sold only to the lender and at a previously determined price. This price is the source of the trader's profit, and accordingly is set well below that at which he expects to resell. How far below varies, of course, and is a matter about which almost no data are available; but economists of the Papaloapan Commission have estimated that discounts of at least 25 per cent are probably the most common.[6]

The funds used to finance these operations are often those of the final buyer. In the lower basin and the semi-urban area particularly, many wholesale houses and processing plants insure their supplies by directly financing the growers or by furnishing credit to the traders. Under the latter refinement, the buyer contracts with a number of traders at the outset of the agricultural cycle for a specified quantity of produce at a given price. Payment is then made on account over the growing season, with the trader using these funds as the basis for his advance-purchase agreements.

If the impediments to progress imposed by such a system have been great, it would be an oversimplification to conclude that the trader's discount is unwarranted. Both his risks and his costs are substantial. In effect, he is called upon to supervise the operations of a host of small producers, and to assemble, grade, and ship their output at harvest time. But whether discounts of the size indicated above are justified is another matter. Generally, each locale is served by just one or two traders, and certainly the less scrupulous among them have not shown themselves indisposed to using their monopoly or near-monopoly positions to dictate artificially low prices. Nor does the manner in which credits are extended have much to commend it. Instead of lending at the outset of the growing season, the traders usually attempt to reduce the risk factor by withholding their advances until after the crop has become well established and then setting their loan quotas at a fraction of the harvest's expected value.[7]

---

[6] One of the few instances for which some direct evidence is available pertains to the tobacco region around Valle Nacional. According to data collected by the Commission, the average advance-purchase price paid by the trader-intermediaries in Tuxtepec during the three years ending with 1956 for filler (*tripa*) leaf was 26.3 pesos per *arroba* (11.5 kilograms), whereas the traders received an average of 42.7 pesos from the manufacturers in Córdoba. If the visible costs of marketing (i.e., those of transportation and handling) are estimated at five pesos per arroba, an apparent discount of 27 per cent results (*23*, Table 7).

[7] There is one important exception to this generalization. Growers of sugar cane in the commercial cropping regions are advanced credit at the outset of the growing season on the basis of five-year contracts with the grinding mills or their intermediaries. Although the circumstances surrounding this credit leave much to be desired from the borrowers' point of view, its availability has been one of the factors behind the recent upsurge in the basin's production of sugar cane.

Though the undesirable effects of advance purchase have been felt everywhere in the basin, the system has probably been most deleterious as it is practiced among the Indians in the interior of the upper basin. So impoverished are the peasants here that many are forced to borrow against their next subsistence crop. Because of the exceptionally high risk under these conditions, many of the traders in the area strengthen their leverage by setting up exclusive "spheres of influence." In the region of the Mazatecs, the more powerful traders have even gone so far as to maintain, with the tacit consent of local and state officials, armed groups of quasi-legal "police" to enforce collection of their loans and to intimidate potential rivals. Against such a preponderence of power the Indian has had little choice but to submit. Indeed, although treatment of the Indian in Mexico has vastly improved since the Revolution, in these particularly isolated areas the concept of debt servitude still has practical meaning (27, pp. 106–7, 129–30).

Some idea of the prevalence of the advance-purchase system in the basin may be had from the meager extent to which alternative sources of production credit have developed. According to a survey of credit practices conducted in the early 1950's, the banks in Córdoba and Veracruz, the principal financial and trading centers for the region, made hardly any loans to the basin's agriculturists, save to the few large cattle ranchers. Instead, these banks loaned chiefly to the processing plants, wholesale houses, or traders, who in turn used the advance-purchase technique to finance the growers (23, pp. 12–13). Nor were the government-operated agricultural banks, the Banco Nacional de Crédito Ejidal and the Banco Nacional de Crédito Agrícola y Ganadero, especially active in the area. For all practical purposes neither extended credit in the hinterland of the upper basin, and during the years of their most intense lending (1953 and 1954) the two together financed not more than a tenth of the harvested area in the lowlands (23, Tables 4, 5).

LAND USE

The agricultural economy of the Papaloapan basin has its basis in both crop and livestock production. It is not, however, an area of

TABLE 3.—PAPALOAPAN BASIN: LAND UTILIZATION, BY REGION, 1949/50*

(Thousand hectares; per cent)

Region	Total Area	Cropland				Pasture		Forest		Other[a]	
		Cultivated		Fallow							
		Area	%	Area	%	Area	%	Area	%	Area	%
Lower basin and Tuxtlas area ..	1,763	166	9	203	12	526	30	505	29	363	20
Upper basin:											
Semi-urban portion	489	118	24	44	9	97	20	24	5	206	42
Hinterland	2,374	185	8	210	9	540	23	888	37	551	23
Total basin ..	4,626	469	10	457	10	1,163	25	1,417	31	1,120	24

* Calculated from Mexico, Sec. Econ., Dir. Gen. Estad., Tercer censo agrícola ganadero y ejidal, 1950. Oaxaca (1956); ibid., Puebla (1958); ibid., Veracruz (1956).

[a] Includes land classified as unproductive, productive but uncultivated, and 670,000 hectares not censused and presumably non-agricultural.

mixed farming. As in the country as a whole, the individual agriculturist is either a cattleman or a crop farmer. Among the crop farmers, moreover, the degree of specialization has been carried even further. Depending on his location, the grower has tended to be either a subsistence farmer producing little or no marketable surplus, or a commercial producer specializing in one particular crop. This threefold breakdown also applies (although with somewhat less validity) to the local patterns of land use.

As would be expected of an area so diverse in its physical and human resources, these local patterns vary greatly. But in very general terms one may say that the lowland is a region of both crop and livestock production, whereas the upper basin is chiefly a crop-producing area (notwithstanding the large proportion of land reported as pasture), and that although subsistence cropping is the rule throughout the basin, an important fringe of commercial growers has developed in the lower basin and in the semi-urban area.

It has already been noted that only a fraction of the basin (about one-third) was given over to some type of cropping or pasture in 1949/50 (Table 3). The concentration of this land is greatest in the semi-urban area. Embracing only a tenth of the basin's territory but almost a third of its population, this region contained fully a quarter of the cultivated land in 1949/50. In that year 25 per cent of its area was reported as planted to either field or tree crops. Crop production here is largely confined to the section corresponding to the windward slope of the Sierra Madre; much of the western third is too dry for non-irrigated cropping, and, where utilized, it is chiefly as pasture.

In the interior, or hinterland, of the upper basin the proportion of cultivated land is much smaller; no more than 8 per cent of the area was cropped in 1949/50. Cultivation is concentrated in the higher, cooler, yet still humid reaches of the Sierra's windward slope and immediately south of the semi-urban section. Elsewhere, the amount of land under cultivation is negligible. The sparsely populated eastern slope region to the southeast of the Santo Domingo remains almost entirely in virgin forest, and much of such cropping as takes place in the rain-shadow portion of the west is confined to scattered irrigated fields in the floor of the Cañada and along the rivulets that

(Thousand hecteres; million pesos)

Region	Total	Corn^a	Sugar cane	Beans^a	Coffee	Rice	Wheat	Bananas	Pineapples	Tobacco	Others
				HARVESTED AREA^b							
Lower basin and Tuxtlas area ..	154.1	67.5	31.8	17.6	2.4	11.7	—	4.4	4.1	2.6	12.0
Upper basin: Semi-urban:											
portion	103.3	55.5	7.8	6.8	10.5	—	3.0	1.8	—	.1	17.8
Hinterland ...	173.4	113.9	8.5	11.9	19.1	.4	8.5	1.6	—	.6	8.9
Total basin .	430.8	236.9	48.1	36.3	32.0	12.1	11.5	7.8	4.1	3.3	38.7
				VALUE OF PRODUCTION							
Lower basin and Tuxtlas area ..	159.3	24.5	54.2	7.9	7.4	6.1	—	7.5	28.2	4.5	19.0
Upper basin: Semi-urban:											
portion	74.5	12.2	10.7	1.5	27.7	—	.9	2.4	.1	.2	18.8
Hinterland ...	109.5	32.6	12.5	4.0	33.7	.2	3.6	3.4	.1	1.3	18.1
Total basin .	343.3	69.3	77.4	13.4	68.8	6.3	4.5	13.3	28.4	6.0	55.9

* Based on Mexico, Sec. Econ., Dir. Gen. Estad., *Tercer censo agrícola ganadero y ejidal, 1950. Oaxaca* (1956); *ibid., Puebla* (1958); *ibid., Veracruz* (1956).

^a Corn area includes area intercultivated with other crops; bean area includes only area on which beans are grown alone.

^b Except for bananas, pineapples, and coffee, which are planted area.

flow into it. A considerable part of this western section is classified as pasture. But so arid is the pasture here, as in the western part of the semi-urban area, and so limited the number of goats and sheep it can carry, that the term is hardly justified.

In the lower basin and the Tuxtlas highlands, with only 9 per cent of their combined area reported as cultivated in 1949/50, the proportion of land in crops is equally small. Here most of the cultivated land, like the population, is localized along the margins of the principal streams (notably the Papaloapan, Tesechoacan, and lower Blanco rivers), in and around the Tuxtlas hills, and, to a somewhat lesser degree, along the railroads. This distribution, as we have noted, chiefly reflects differences in soil quality; the alluvial soils of the river margins and the volcanic soils of the Tuxtlas area are considerably more fertile than the lateritic soils found in the interfluvial plains. Outside the areas along the railroads these plains are virtually devoid of cultivated land save for a few widely scattered plots. But, unlike the bulk of the uncultivated territory in the upper basin, they are not totally unexploited. A substantial portion, comprising the only true livestock region of the basin, is given over to cattle grazing, albeit in a very extensive basis.

Cropping Patterns

Although the basin is capable of growing an immense variety of crops, an extremely small number occupy most of the cultivated land and contribute the greater part of the gross value of output (Table 4). The six leading crops—corn, sugar cane, beans, coffee, rice, and wheat —occupied 88 per cent of the harvested area in 1949/50, and corn alone 55 per cent. Together with beans, the other basic component of the traditional diet of the Mexican peasant, corn is grown as a subsistence crop everywhere in the basin. The proportion of land devoted to it attests to the area's economic backwardness.[8]

[8] The importance of corn to the basin's subsistence farmers, especially those in the interior of the upper basin, cannot be stressed too strongly. In the more isolated settlements, all other crops are wholly subordinate to it. Though no detailed dietary survey has as yet been made in any of these regions, the limited qualitative evidence consistently suggests that the proportion of available calories supplied by corn is well over the 50 per cent estimated for the Mexican people as a whole. With reference to the Indians inhabiting the slopes of Mt. Zempoaltepec, for instance, Ralph Beals

Because of differences in the unit value of output, however, area figures alone do not accurately reflect the relative contribution of the various crops to the basin's agricultural economy. In terms of value of production, the three dominant crops are sugar cane, corn, and coffee (63 per cent of the value of all crops in 1949/50), followed by pineapples, beans, bananas, rice, and tobacco (20 per cent of the 1949/50 crop valuation). Just as the proportion of land in corn suggests the comparative importance of subsistence agriculture, the value ranking indicates the type and location of the basin's commercial crop production. Of the major crops grown chiefly for the market, sugar cane, pineapples, bananas, and tobacco are products of the tierra caliente, while only coffee is an upland crop.

The principal areas of commercial production are shown in Map 9. This map clearly illustrates the crucial role played by transportation in determining the location of commercial output. With the single exception of coffee, a high unit-value commodity that can be transported economically even under primitive conditions, the production of commercial crops is almost entirely located along the railroads and navigable streams of the lower basin and the semi-urban region.

Of the various crops grown commercially, sugar cane ranks first in both area under exploitation and value of output. In 1949/50 it occupied 11 per cent of the harvested area and contributed almost 25 per cent of the value of crop production. Production is heavily concentrated in three regions: along the banks of the Papaloapan, around Lerdo de Tejada and Cuatotolapan at the base of the Tuxtlas highlands, and along the Orizaba—Acatlán portion of the Ferrocarril Mexicano and Córdoba–Jesús Carranza rail lines. In these areas cane is grown almost exclusively. For example, in the municipality of Amatitlán,[9] on the western margin of the Papaloapan between the

---

states that "the background of Mixe life is dominated by maize. Maize is the object of most of Mixe labor. It is the principal food, to which all other foods are in the relation of condiments or occasional luxuries. Days and weeks may pass without other nutriment than that derived from maize. If the maize crop succeeds, there is plenty; if it fails utterly, there is famine, perhaps death" (5, p. 100).

[9] The only municipality (the smallest census unit) small enough to fall entirely within one of the sugar areas.

towns of San Cristóbal and Tlacotalpan, the 1950 Census reported 93 per cent of the harvested area in sugar. These regions, taken together, make up the most important sugar zone of Mexico. For at least the last 25 years the basin has consistently accounted for over a quarter of the Republic's cane output (*8*, vol. I, pp. 267–70).

Insofar as processing facilities are concerned, there are 17 sugar mills in the basin, at least one in each of the producing areas. Most of these mills are small and inefficient, however, and with the recent improvement in transport facilities under the Papaloapan Project there has been a marked tendency for the few larger plants to grind a progressively greater portion of the harvest. During the 1957/58 season, five mills ground 72 per cent of the crop; the San Cristóbal mill alone ground 43 per cent (*19*, p. 258). By far the largest mill in Mexico, San Cristóbal claimed to have ground more cane during the 1954/55 season than any other mill in the world—1.4 million metric tons—and since then its output has been boosted sharply (*7*, p. 10-A).

The specialization of crops in the other areas of commercial production is considerably less pronounced than in the sugar regions. This is particularly true of the three small areas along the Córdoba–Jesús Carranza railroad that grow the bulk of the basin's pineapples, in value terms the second-ranking market crop of the lowlands. Although the pineapple is far and away the most important crop of these regions, it occupies only a fraction of the area in farms because it is intensively cultivated on a comparatively small acreage. As in the surrounding regions of grazing and subsistence cropping, corn, beans, rice, and pasture occupy most of the agricultural land.

In contrast to the areas devoted to pineapple and sugar-cane production, which have expanded rapidly in the past several decades, the area devoted to bananas, in value terms the third most important market crop of the lowlands, has suffered a marked reduction. The present commercial banana region around Tuxtepec is a small remnant of that which existed during the 1930's, when Mexico was one of the world's largest producers of export bananas, and when, together with the Grijalva area of Tabasco State, the basin produced most of the crop. At that time, Gros Michel bananas were widely grown along the rivers in the more humid sections of the lowlands, and were probably the basin's leading market crop (*3*, p. 96).

As in so many other regions that once grew bananas for export, the period of banana primacy in the basin was brief, spanning little more than a decade. Following the introduction in the mid-1920's of the Gros Michel variety, on which the export trade is based, the area in bananas increased rapidly. The appearance of sigatoka disease (*Cercospora musae*) in 1938 spelled the downfall of the industry. A fungus disease that deprives the plant of its vigor and results in progressively smaller stems of fruit, sigatoka had played havoc in the banana areas of Central America a few years previously. In these regions the large fruit companies were eventually able to control it by massive spraying programs, but in the basin the high cost of the necessary equipment proved beyond the means of even the largest growers.[10] Left unchecked, the disease spread at an alarming rate. Output fell drastically. In 1940/41 the harvest amounted to less than half that of the previous year, and the Standard Fruit Company, which since 1923 had purchased the greater part of the basin's output, suspended operations in the area (*3*, p. 98; *20*, p. 90; *12*, pp. 388–89).

By 1950 production of the Gros Michel variety had all but ceased, most of the land formerly in bananas having been planted to sugar cane or subsistence crops. Only in the small area around Tuxtepec has the banana industry been continued on any scale. The varieties now grown are disease resistant, but since these varieties have no place in world trade, production is now exclusively for the limited and less profitable domestic market.

Because of their modest size, the two regions specializing in the growing of tobacco, in terms of both value and area the least important of the four major market crops of the lowlands, are not indicated in Map 9. Both regions are situated at the base of the Sierra Madre, one along the Valle Nacional River near the town of the same name,

---

[10] The inability of the basin's producers to take steps to control the spread of sigatoka was also related to the fact that the disease struck at precisely the moment the country was in the midst of its great agrarian reform. For the growers, their associations, and the large foreign buyers to have achieved the degree of cooperation necessary for the institution of preventive measures at such a time would have been just about impossible.

the other on the margins of the Tesechoacan near Playa Vicente. Together they accounted for well over two-thirds of the 3,300 hectares devoted to the crop in 1949/50.

As with bananas, the area presently given over to tobacco is only a fraction of what was once under cultivation. One of the few commodities grown commercially in the basin before the rail system was completed, tobacco achieved its greatest importance around the turn of the century. Such meager (and none too reliable) statistical evidence as is available for this period suggests that output was then at least double its recent level, and that both the Córdoba and Tuxtlas areas as well as the Valle Nacional region were important growers (18, pp. 497, 545). At that time production was oriented toward the export market, with most of the harvest composed of high-quality filler leaf for cigars. But during the following decade quality was permitted to deteriorate in favor of higher yields, and the industry was in full decline when the Revolution of 1910 disrupted production. Although planting began again on a modest scale during the 1930's, the limited domestic market for poor-quality cigar leaf has prevented anything approaching full recovery (1, pp. 1–2).

In comparison with the major commercial crops of the lowlands, which are almost exclusively grown within four or five miles of the railroads or navigable streams, coffee, the only important market crop of the upland portions of the basin, is produced rather widely. With respect to both area under cultivation and value of output, it is second only to sugar cane as the basin's leading commercial crop, and is found throughout the populated sections of the Sierra's windward slope. This is not to say that, because of coffee's high unit value, location of production has not been influenced by availability of transport. Of the 32,000 hectares planted to coffee in 1949/50, almost two-thirds were situated in the semi-urban region around Córdoba and in the Zongolica area immediately to the south. Moreover, the greater part of the remainder is localized in the vicinity of Huautla and Ojitlán, where, although transportation is difficult, the distance to the railroads is comparatively short. In the other areas the plantings are not only widely scattered but production is often more subsistence than commercial in character.

Except in these more isolated regions, the basin's coffee is produced for the export market. Mild *arabica* coffees are grown almost exclusively, and considerable attention is given to adequate shading and hand selection of mature berries. Quality, nevertheless, varies greatly. The coffees of the Córdoba and Zongolica regions are carefully processed and command premium prices. Those of the interior regions, on the other hand, are typically prepared under primitive conditions, and commonly sell at a substantial discount.

Grazing

The contribution of livestock and livestock products to the basin's agricultural economy is decidedly secondary to that of crop production. For the area as a whole, the value of livestock production amounted to only 30 per cent of all farm output in 1949/50 (Tables 5 and 6). But since the regional importance of grazing differs sharply, such an over-all comparison is not particularly instructive. If the contribution of livestock is negligible in the upper basin, in the lowlands cattle raising is one of the chief sources of farm income.

The lower basin has been an important livestock region for well over 400 years. Encouraged by liberal land grants but lacking an indigenous basis for estate agriculture, the Spanish began introducing cattle into the area almost immediately after the Conquest. The results, we are told, were nothing short of spectacular. Within a few decades the production of cattle had become firmly established, and

TABLE 5.—PAPALOAPAN BASIN: NUMBER OF LIVESTOCK, BY REGION, 1949/50*

(Thousand head)

Region	Cattle	Swine	Goats and sheep	Fowl
Lower basin and Tuxtlas area	407	193	14	1,573
Upper basin:				
Semi-urban portion	42	41	124	588
Hinterland	89	87	236	1,038
Total basin	538	321	374	3,199

TABLE 6.—PAPALOAPAN BASIN: ESTIMATED VALUE OF LIVESTOCK
PRODUCTION, BY REGION, 1949/50*

(Million pesos)

		Livestock				Livestock products		
	Total	Cattle	Swine	Goats and Sheep	Fowl	Dairy Products	Eggs	Other
Lower basin and Tuxtlas area	93.9	29.5	6.4	.2	5.0	37.8	14.5	.6
Upper basin: Semi-urban portion	22.1	3.8	1.6	1.2	1.9	7.4	5.8	.3
Hinterland	36.6	5.7	3.1	2.0	3.5	13.2	8.7	.5
Total basin	152.5	39.0	11.1	3.4	10.4	58.4	28.9	1.3

* Tables 5 and 6 are calculated from Mexico, Sec. Econ., Dir. Gen. Estad., *Tercer censo agrícola ganadero y ejidal, 1950. Oaxaca* (1956); *ibid., Puebla* (1958); *ibid., Veracruz* (1956).
Livestock numbers and value of livestock products are taken directly from the 1950 Census of Agriculture. Because this census does not include data on the number and value of livestock sold or slaughtered, the values for livestock production are estimates. Except for sheep, for which no evidence was given (other than that the proportion is very low) and for which 33 per cent was arbitrarily taken (considering the meager worth of the wool clip, this rate makes the census value of sheep appear reasonable), the proportion of total stock that was slaughtered or sold annually was estimated on the basis of qualitative and quantitative indicators in José Attolini, *Economía de la cuenca del Papaloapan: Bosques, fauna, pesca, ganadería e industria* (México, D.F., 1950): 21 per cent for cattle (p. 60); 33 per cent for swine (p. 71); 42 per cent for goats (pp. 66, 104, 106); 55 per cent for fowl (p. 75). The resulting figures were multiplied by the average census value of stock in the census age category nearest that at which the animals are typically sold or slaughtered (the age categories used were: over 3 years for cattle; over 1 year for swine; and 6 months to 2 years for goats) except in the cases of sheep and fowl, for which the average value of all head was used. Horses, asses, mules, and other work stock omitted.

by 1600 it is said to have occupied virtually all of the area's more openly vegetated land (*29*, pp. 280–81).

For most of the next three centuries the coastal plain was essentially a great cattle range. During this period, which saw the bulk of Mexico's agricultural land fall under the control of the latifundia system, most of its territory passed into large cattle haciendas. Since prestige was then often as powerful a motive for land ownership as profit, the estate owners were commonly content with the relatively small returns to be had from ranching, and rarely attempted to devote their holdings to more remunerative uses. Cropping was largely restricted to the small plots of landless peasants who were permitted, under what is known in Latin America as the *colono* system, to plant two or three hectares of estate land to subsistence crops in exchange for being available as workers. Cattle production, however, continued to expand, and it is estimated that the lower basin contained between 300,000 and 500,000 head by the latter part of the nineteenth century (*29*, p. 281).

Since that time the importance of grazing relative to crop production has steadily declined. This trend, evident soon after completion of the rail system, was greatly hastened by the post-Revolutionary land reform, which saw much of the better land along the rivers taken over by ejidos and converted into small crop farms. This is not to imply that the number of cattle has diminished; despite a sharp drop during and after the Revolution, it has continued to increase.[11] But, while grazing still occupies the greater part of the agricultural land in the coastal plain, in terms of both value of output and number of persons engaged it has been superseded by crop farming. Only in the thinly settled interfluvial areas is livestock production still the principal occupation.

In these areas ranching is carried on much as it was during the pre-Revolutionary period. Although the old haciendas are gone, the bulk of the land remains in a few large private holdings which continue to pasture cattle on an extensive basis. An idea of the size and number of these ranches may be had from the fact that in 1949/50 the 773 ranches with more than 200 hectares each controlled roughly 700,000 hectares, or almost half the territory of the lower basin. And of this area, approximately 500,000 hectares were controlled by no more than 270 estates, each with at least 500 hectares.

For the most part, the cattle are grazed on natural pasture of Bermuda and grama grass in tracts that have only been partially cleared. In a few sections, however, planted pasture of Pará or Guinea grass

---

[11] This statement would at first glance appear to be at variance with the estimate of cattle numbers reported in the 1950 Census (see Table 5). This is most probably not the case. Official livestock data in Mexico are notoriously inaccurate and commonly understate by a considerable margin. There is reason to believe that the degree of understatement was especially great in the 1950 Census, taken in the midst of a governmental campaign to eradicate foot-and-mouth disease by slaughtering all ruminants that had been exposed to it, making many cattlemen particularly anxious to conceal their true holdings. Indeed, in 1957 the livestock producers of Veracruz admitted as much, and called for a new census (*25*, p. 22).

has been introduced in scattered clearings. But under present management the carrying capacity of such planted pasture is not much greater than that of the natural pasture: the average for both is variously estimated at between 1.0 and 2.8 hectares per mature animal (*29*, p. 285; *21*, p. 10). Yet cattle ranching is even more extensive than these carrying capacities would suggest. Except in the more humid localities near the base of the Sierra, the length and intensity of the dry season have determined a semi-nomadic type of grazing, with a given tract of land rarely utilized more than eight months out of the year.[12]

In general, the quality of the animals pastured in the lower basin is poor. Despite recent efforts to introduce purebred bulls into the area, the majority of the cattle still consist of light and rangy crosses of degenerated native stock (*criollo*) and Zebu, which, while raised for both milk and beef, are effcient producers of neither. They are generally marketed locally, Veracruz and Córdoba-Orizaba being the principal buying centers.

LAND TENURE AND RURAL UNDEREMPLOYMENT

Size of Holdings

The regional importance of Mexico's three general systems of land tenure—the pre-Cortesian communal system, the individual private holding introduced by the Spaniards, and the ejido system of the post-Revolutionary land reform—differs greatly within the Papaloapan basin (Table 7). In the hinterland of the upper basin, one of the few sections of the country where geography was such as to enable the indigenous population to successfully resist Spanish attempts at subjugation, almost two-thirds of the land is still held under

---

[12] The following system of transhumance is generally practiced. During the rainy period the cattle are kept on relatively high land away from the rivers. As the dry season progresses, the pasture begins to dry out and lose much of its nutritional value. During March–April and earlier months the cattle are driven to lower-lying areas, notably the semi-swamp regions behind the Laguna de Alvarado and along the lower reaches of the Tesechoacan and San Juan rivers, where soil moisture is adequate throughout the year. Here they remain until about mid-July, when water intrusion forces them back to higher terrain (*29*, pp. 285–86).

The regions of dry-season pasture roughly approximate those shown in Map 9 as subject to seasonal flooding or water intrusion.

TABLE 7.—PAPALOAPAN BASIN: LAND OWNERSHIP,
BY REGION, 1949/50*

(*Thousand hectares; per cent*)

Region	Total area	Private		Communal		Ejidal		Other[a]	
		Area	%	Area	%	Area	%	Area	%
Lower basin and Tuxtlas area ..	1,763	939	53	16	1	526	30	281	16
Upper basin: Semi-urban portion	489	117	24	3	1	190	39	178	36
Hinterland	2,374	392	17	1,452	61	264	11	267	11
Total basin	4,626	1,448	31	1,471	32	980	21	726	16

* Calculated from Mexico, Sec. Econ., Dir. Gen. Estad., *Tercer censo agrícola ganadero y ejidal, 1950. Oaxaca* (1956); *ibid., Puebla* (1958); *ibid., Veracruz* (1956).

[a] Includes land reported as owned by both the federal and state governments, plus 670,000 hectares that were not censused. For evidence to support an assumption that this uncensused land was almost entirely owned by the federal government, see Armando González Santos, *La Agricultura: Estructura y utilización de los recursos* (México, D.F., and Buenos Aires, 1957), pp. 16–17, 45.

the communal system. Essentially a carry-over of the pre Cortesian landholding village, this system calls for title to be vested in the community and the use of land to be administered by its elected officials. In practice, however, communal ownership has come to imply individual tenure by right of use. Each *comunero* (member of a landholding village) is free to utilize any unoccupied plot he desires, and it is treated as his so long as he chooses to exploit it (5, p. 101).

In the lower basin and the semi-urban region, the landholding village has long been a negligible factor; almost all of the agricultural land, as in the country as a whole, was absorbed into a few private holdings during the colonial period and the first century of independence. It was in these regions, consequently, that the post-Revolutionary pressures for reform were the greatest and that the ejido system has achieved its chief importance. Although little land was expropriated and formed into ejidos before 1935, the amount of property transferred in the next few years was substantial. By 1949/50 almost a third of the land in the two regions had been granted to some 700 ejidos, with a total of about 50,000 ejidatorios having received plots. In that year 66 and 55 per cent of the cultivated area in the lowlands and in the semi-urban portion, respectively, were included in ejidos. Only in the sparsely populated grazing areas of the interfluvial plains did the old estates emerge comparatively unscathed.[13]

Save for the large ranches in this one region, the typical holding throughout the basin, whether it be private, communal, or ejidal, is now very small. Just how small it is not possible to determine. Except for private properties, the decennial censuses do not report breakdowns according to farm size. Nevertheless, given the preeminence of crop agriculture other than in the interfluvial plains, one can gain a fairly accurate impression of the amount of land actually under exploitation in the typical unit, both over time and yearly, by dividing the areas reported as "crop land" (i.e., that cultivated in the census year or in any of the previous five) and as "cultivated" by the number of units reported. For 1949/50, as the following tabulation reveals, such calculations indicate that the basin's 166,000 holdings contained an average of only 5.6 hectares of crop land and a mere 2.8 hectares under cultivation:[14]

Region	Number of holdings	Hectares per average holding	
		Crop land	Cultivated land
Lower basin and Tuxtlas area	39,886	9.2	4.2
Upper basin:			
Semi-urban portion	49,656	3.2	2.4
Hinterland	76,342	5.2	2.4
Total basin	165,884	5.6	2.8

[13] Although it has been well over a decade since any appreciable amount of land in the basin has been expropriated for incorporation into ejidos, the large private holdings in the interfluvial plains are not out of jeopardy. If they exceed certain maximum sizes, as many of the larger ones do, they are still liable to expropriation "for reasons of public interest" at the pleasure of the government, especially if a sufficiently large landless peasantry should develop in their environs and petition for redistribution. According to present legislation, the maximum area a private holding may contain free of the fear of expropriation varies with its quality and the use to which it is put: 100 hectares for irrigated or "humid" crop land; 200 hectares for seasonal crop land or cultivable pasture; 300 hectares for land planted to such perennials as bananas, sugar cane, coffee, rubber, or fruit trees; or enough pasture land (about 500 hectares in the lower basin) to support the equivalent of 500 head of cattle (28, p. 218).

[14] Computed from data in Tables 3 and 8. The number of holdings, for which an

While these data suggest that fragmentation of agricultural land has been carried even further in the basin than in Mexico as a whole —the national average in the same year was 7.3 hectares of crop land and 4.0 hectares under cultivation per holding (see Chapter 2)— they also indicate rather marked regional disparities. By either measure the exploited area per holding in both the interior and the semi-urban portions of the upper basin fell markedly short of the national average, whereas in the lowlands it was slightly greater. This difference can be explained in part by the fact that some of the land included in the large cattle estates is given over to cropping. But even if these units are excluded from consideration, the exploited area of the typical farm in the coastal plain would still appear to be about half again that in the upper basin. Discounting the 270 largest ranches, which, with a combined area of 550,000 hectares, controlled the greater part of the territory of the interfluvial plains, the remaining 39,616 units still contained an average of 7.2 hectares of crop land.

Rural Underemployment

In view of the pre-eminence of minifundia throughout most of the basin and the nature of the tenure systems under which they are held, it comes as no surprise that the agricultural labor force is composed chiefly of holder-operators and members of their families. Nor is it surprising, given the extremely limited area under cultivation in the typical farm, that per capita earnings are low and underemployment widespread. Although statistical shortcomings again make any precise quantitative appraisal impossible (the evidence contained in the decennial censuses is both meager and conflicting), Table 8 sheds some light on these points.

This table suggests that the landless laborer is no longer a major factor in Papaloapan agriculture. Fully 98 per cent of the farm units were holder-operated in 1949/50, and between 80 and 90 per cent (depending on which census estimate is used) of the persons engaged

---

incomplete figure is given in the census, is taken as being equal to the number of farm operators.

in agricultural pursuits were either holder-operators or members of their families. To be sure, a small body of landless workers still remains (how small it is impossible to determine), but the fact that there is no evidence of renewed pressure for breaking up the large cattle ranches would seem to indicate that the numbers are negligible (*22*, p. 165).

As to the prevalence of underemployment, the tenuous evidence that is available is less favorable. The amount of double counting indicated in Table 8 suggests that about 20 per cent of the farm-labor force in 1949/50 added to their income by taking second jobs, typically as seasonal day laborers on neighboring commercial holdings, after caring for their own units. Most persons in this group (55 per cent) lived in the semi-urban region, where commercial production is most concentrated and where the opportunities for part-time farm work are most numerous; over 40 per cent of that area's rural work force held more than one job. The implication is that had similar opportunities been available in the rest of the basin, an equally high proportion there would also have taken supplemental employment off the farm.

This reasoning suggests that rural underemployment is chronic throughout the basin. It does not follow, however, that the prime cause of underemployment is the small size of the typical holding. Were this the case, one would expect that the larger amount of land exploited in the average holding in the lowlands would be reflected by something approaching a proportional increase in the area exploited per worker, and, as the following tabulation (for 1949/50) indicates, this does not obtain:[15]

Region	Agricultural labor force	Average no. of workers per unit	Average cultivated area per worker (*hectares*)
Lower basin and Tuxtlas area	90,910	2.3	1.8
Upper basin:			
Semi-urban portion	61,232	1.2	1.9
Hinterland	107,436	1.4	1.7
Total basin	259,578	1.6	1.8

[15] Computed from data in Tables 3 and 8.

TABLE 8.—PAPALOAPAN BASIN: COMPOSITION OF AGRICULTURAL LABOR FORCE, BY REGION, 1949/50*

(Thousands)

| Region | Agricultural labor force (Census of Agriculture) | | | | | | | | | Agricultural labor force (Census of Population) | Apparent double counting |
| | Farm Operators | | | | | Day laborers | Unpaid family help | Others | Total | | |
	Private holders	Ejida-tarios	Comu-neros^a	Share-croppers	Sub-total						
Lower basin and Tuxtlas area	9.0	29.2	1.2	.5	39.9	29.0	30.7	2.9	102.4	90.9	11.5
Upper basin:											
Semi-urban portion	28.8	19.7	—	1.1	49.6	16.1	20.2	.2	86.2	61.2	25.0
Hinterland	47.3	11.2	17.5	.3	76.3	23.3	17.1	.1	116.8	107.4	9.4
Total basin ...	85.1	60.1	18.7	1.9	165.8	68.4	68.0	3.2	305.4	259.5	45.9

* Based on Mexico, Sec. Econ., Dir. Gen. Estad., *Septimo censo general de población, Estado de Oaxaca* (1953); *ibid., Estado de Puebla* (1953); *ibid., Estado de Veracruz* (1953); Mexico, Sec. Econ., Dir. Gen. Estad., *Tercer censo agrícola ganadero y ejidal, 1950. Oaxaca* (1956); *ibid., Puebla* (1958); and *ibid., Veracruz* (1956).

It should be noted that this table contains two conflicting estimates of the size of the basin's agricultural labor force in 1949/50. The chief cause of the conflict lies in the different reporting procedures employed in the two censuses cited. The Population Census reported the number of persons who gave agriculture as their principal occupation as of June 6, 1950, whereas the Agricultural Census enumerated on a farm-by-farm basis all persons who actively contributed to production during the May 1949/April 1950 crop year. Thus the latter reported a gross estimate, and double counted those individuals who worked on more than one farm. But, if the Population Census figures represent the better estimates of total numbers, an occupational breakdown is given only for the Agricultural Census total. If they are to serve as bases for valid conclusions about the size and composition of the basin's farm labor force, therefore, the estimates of the two censuses must be utilized in conjunction.

ᵃ Taken to be those reported as "others" in municipalities with communal holdings.

Instead, the amount of land exploited per worker is equally small throughout the basin, the greater size of the typical holding in the lowlands being completely offset by a rise in the number of workers occupied per unit. This indicates that the principal cause of agricultural underemployment lies not so much in artificial restrictions imposed by farm size, but in the nature of the systems of production— systems which in themselves decisively limit the amount of land an individual can effectively exploit.

SYSTEMS OF PRODUCTION

The systems of farming prevailing in the basin, as in the other more isolated sections of Mexico, have improved but slightly over time. For the most part, agriculture continues to be both a primitive and a labor-intensive operation, with the machete, digging stick, and wooden plow persisting as the principal implements. Modern techniques, though not unknown, are restricted almost entirely to the operations of a few of the most progressive commercial growers. There were only 278 tractors in the entire basin in 1949/50, 212 of them in the lowlands, and a mere 3.5 per cent of the cultivated area was treated with commercial fertilizer.

Except in the rain-shadow portion of the western uplands, where low rainfall has determined a sedentary (and often irrigated) agriculture, crop production is still dominated by the age-old system of fire agriculture and shifting cultivation. Known locally as *roza y quema* ("slash and burn"), this system is essentially the same as that practiced throughout most of the world's sparsely populated humid tropics. Clearing and burning alone prepare the land for cropping, and a given plot is exploited on a temporary basis. After one, two, or, at most, three years, a combination of weed intrusion and fertility exhaustion reduces yields to an uneconomic level and forces abandonment; a new plot is then cleared and the previous one returned to "bush fallow." Although the plow is now quite commonly used in the basin, especially in the more advanced commercial cropping regions, it has typically been superimposed on this system, rather than substituted for it.

Fire Agriculture

The basic system of fire farming practiced in the basin can perhaps most clearly be summarized with reference to the following generalized calendar of operations for the leading crop, spring-sown corn (adapted from *3*, pp. 42–47):

Operation	Month	Implements used	Man days per hectare
Clearing	February–April	Axe and machete	15–20[16]
Burning	May	—	4
Planting	May–June	Digging stick	5
Cleanings (two)	June–August	Machete or *tarpala*[17]	20
Bending[18]	September	—	2
Cleaning[19]	September	Machete or *tarpala*	10
Harvesting	October–January	—	8

Preparation of a new plot begins about midway through the dry season. At that time the plot is selected and completely cleared of vegetation. This is the most time-consuming task involved in the preparation, and consequently is chiefly responsible for the small amount of land exploited per holding. With an average of from 15 to 20 man-days of labor required to clear a hectare of land with implements no more effective than the machete and axe, few families can prepare more than two or three hectares each season.

Once the plot has been cleared, the rubble is left to dry for a month or so, and then burned. Burning is usually delayed until a few days before the onset of the summer rains, and is followed within a week or two by planting. In the planting operation, the digging stick, a pointed sapling some six feet long and one or two inches in diameter, is the only implement used. Corn is planted in hills approximately three feet apart. As the peasant steps off this distance, he punches a hole with his stick, drops in a few seeds, and covers them over with soil. After the crop has been planted, it receives very little attention

---

[16] Varies with length of time land has been in bush fallow.

[17] A hoe-like tool with its blade set in line with the handle.

[18] Because in the more humid portions of the basin corn matures before the end of the rainy period, the stalk must be bent to prevent excessive damage from rotting or birds.

[19] Only if a dry-season crop is to be planted.

until harvest time. The field is "cleaned" one or two times—i.e., the weeds are cut back with a machete or tarpala—but otherwise it is largely ignored. The harvest is, of course, collected by hand.

Whether the same clearing is planted again in the fall depends on its location. In the higher sections of the Sierra, corn does not mature until well into the autumn months, when it is too cool for a second crop. But in the more humid portions of the tierra caliente (the lower reaches of the Sierra and the Tuxtlas highlands, and the western margin of the coastal plain) a dry-season crop is frequently attempted. Since this crop is often planted before the end of the rains, and hence before the summer crop is harvested, it is not preceded by burning. In the common lowland sequence of fall-sown beans following spring-sown corn, the area between corn rows is merely cleaned before the beans are planted.

In the upper basin a field is rarely cultivated two years in succession under this system. Despite fair initial returns, the thin mountain soils here are quickly exhausted or eroded, and are customarily abandoned after only one crop has been taken (5, p. 100). In the lowlands, however, a given plot is usually planted for one or two more years before being returned to natural cover (29, p. 222). In this event, the spring clearing operation during succeeding years is comparatively simple. About all that is required is that the remnants of the previous crop be cut down, piled, and burned, a process demanding only about six man-days per hectare (3, p. 45). Weed intrusion, however, becomes progressively more serious after the first year, and the labor saved in clearing is largely offset by increased cleaning requirements. In the case of corn, the field must be cleaned at least three times between planting and harvesting if the crop is not to be completely taken over by weeds.

Notwithstanding this extra effort, the decline in yields is generally quite rapid after the first year. In the areas around Playa Vicente and Acayucan, for instance, it is estimated that corn yields drop by as much as 50 per cent during the second year (3, p. 16). Whether this decline is due more to the rapid leaching and organic decomposition associated with tropical soils once they have been cleared or to the inability of periodic hand cleanings to prevent the intrusion of weeds has not been resolved, though in the areas of rich alluvial soil it is probably the latter. The effect, in any event, is to compel abandonment after only two or, at most, three years of cropping. Once abandoned, a field is not recleared and planted until it has rested for at least two years, and more generally about five or six (5, p. 103; 29, p. 222).

Plow Agriculture

The system of plow agriculture most commonly practised in the basin is little more than a variation of the basic system of fire farming.[20] Although the field is plowed before planting and the plow is substituted for the machete in the cleaning operation, its other characteristics remain essentially the same. Hand clearing and burning still ready the field for cultivation, and the rotation of fields rather than crops is still customary.[21] Nevertheless, it does represent an important step forward. Because the plow, even the wooden, ox-drawn one typical of all but the most advanced sections of the basin, is a far more efficient implement than the machete for combating weeds, its use substantially lengthens the economic life of a given clearing.

Plowing is not practicable until tree stumps and roots have been removed, and since this is most readily done after they have rotted for some months, a newly cleared plot is rarely cultivated under the plow system. Instead, the first crop is usually taken by the traditional method, and the stumps removed during the succeeding dry season. Once this is done, the generalized calendar of operations, again with spring-sown corn as the example, is as follows (adapted from 3, pp. 41–47):

[20] There are no data to indicate what portion of the basin's cultivated area is exploited with the plow. But the number of plows reported in the 1950 Census, 84,000, suggests that the plow was used on only about half the holdings in that year.

[21] Plowing in connection with field crops is now associated with more or less continuous use of the same field only in the drier portions of the upper basin. But in the more progressive commercial cropping areas of the tierra caliente (notably the sugar regions along the margins of the Papaloapan and in the semi-urban area) the adoption of the steel plow has so lengthened a field's productive life that agriculture has become more sedentary than shifting in character.

Operation	Month	Implements used	Man days per hectare	Days of plow use per hectare
Clearing	April–May	Machete	5	—
Burning	April–May	—	1	—
Plowing[22]	May–June	Plow	12	12
Planting	May–June	Digging stick	3	—
Cleanings (two) ..	June–July	Plow	12	6
Bending	September	—	2	—
Cleaning[23]	September	Plow	6	3
Harvesting	October–January	—	8	—

As with the traditional system, the cycle begins each spring with the cutting down and burning of the preceding crop. (Stalks and stubble are rarely turned under, either because of custom or because it is difficult to do so with a wooden plow; equally uncommon, except among a few of the most progressive cane and pineapple growers, is the use of commercial fertilizers.) This done, the field is plowed, cross-plowed, and, just before planting, furrowed. The digging stick is still used for planting. Cleaning, however, is done with the plow, and is generally a two-man operation. One man guides the ox and plow up and down each row while the second follows behind to right the plants overturned by the ox. Harvesting, again, is done by hand.

The advantage of this system over the traditional one lies primarily in the ability of the plow to control the intrusion of weeds more effectively, and hence to extend the productive life of a clearing. Plowing is also associated with somewhat higher initial yields and larger family plots, but the gains here are slight. In the case of corn, the initial increase in yields is almost entirely offset by a rise in production costs(*11*, pp. 50–52), while, as the above calendar indicates, the labor saved in cleaning with a plow is largely offset by an increase in the time spent preparing the field for planting. The number of years added to the life of a clearing, however, is significant, but varies considerably with soil quality and the crop grown. Fields planted to pineapples under this system in the lowlands are generally not abandoned until after five years, and the most fertile alluvial soils planted

[22] Includes cross-plowing and furrowing.
[23] Only if dry-season crop is to be planted.

to sugar cane are cultivated for as many as eight consecutive years
(*3*, pp. 111, 123).

Per Capita Productivity

Given the small amount of land an individual can exploit under
either of these systems and the predominance of subsistence crops, it
follows that the productivity of the basin's agriculture as expressed
by the value of output per worker is low. Some indication of the seriousness of this situation is revealed in the following tabulation for
1949/50:[24]

	Value of output per worker (*pesos*)			
Region	Total	Crops	Livestock	Livestock products
Lower basin and Tuxtlas area	2,785	1,752	452	581
Upper basin:				
Semi-urban portion	1,577	1,217	141	219
Hinterland	1,360	1,019	133	208
Total basin	1,910	1,323	246	341
Mexico	1,795	1,025	289	481

In that year, the gross value of production per worker amounted to
only 1,910 pesos, or the equivalent at the then prevailing rate of
exchange of a mere $220.

If this figure suggests that per capita output was somewhat greater
than in Mexico as a whole, the tabulation also indicates sharp regional
disparities. In both sections of the upper basin, per capita output fell
considerably short of the national average, whereas in the lowlands
it was over half again as great. The reason for this difference lies not
only in the larger number of livestock raised in the lower basin and
in the more widespread production of such relatively remunerative
crops as pineapples and sugar cane, but also in higher average yields.
Yields in the lowlands, though small, especially on the alluvial soils,
are quite good by Mexican standards. In 1949/50, the only year for

[24] Figures for the Papaloapan basin and its sub-regions computed from data in
Tables 4, 5, 6, and 8. National averages computed from data taken directly from *13*,
p. 60 and *16*, p. 208, except that the value of livestock output, for which no census
figure is given, was estimated by following the same procedures outlined in the foot-
note to Tables 5 and 6.

which statistics are available for a regional comparison, corn returned an average of 1,165 kilograms per hectare (about 18 bushels per acre) in the lowlands, whereas in the upper basin and in the country as a whole, the average yields were only 878 and 790, respectively (*16*, pp. 85, 88). Nevertheless, save for a few cattle ranchers and large-scale commercial growers, the farm population even here could look forward to little but a meager existence from the land.

CITATIONS

1 Roxana Arce Ybarra, "El problema del tabaco en el Valle Nacional" (Comisión del Papaloapan, July 1954, unpublished).

2 Roxana Arce Ybarra, "La navigación fluvial en el sistema del río Papaloapan" (Comisión del Papaloapan, March 1955, unpublished).

3 José Attolini, *Economía de la cuenca del Papaloapan: Agricultura* (México, D.F., 1949).

4 José Attolini, *Economía de la cuenca del Papaloapan: Bosques, fauna, pesca, ganadería e industria* (México, D.F., 1950).

5 R. L. Beals, *Ethnology of the Western Mixe* (Univ. of Calif. Publications in American Archaeology and Ethnology, vol. 42, no. 1, 1945).

6 Fernando Cámara, *Chacaltianguis: Comunidad rural en la ribera del Papaloapan*, vol. I (Gobierno del Estado de Veracruz, 1952).

7 *Excelsior* (México, D.F.), Aug. 3, 1955.

8 Ford, Bacon & Davis, Inc., *La industria azucarera de México*, 3 vols. (Banco de México, S. A., México, D.F., 1952–55).

9 Higgins Industries, Inc., *Estudio sobre México*, part 1 (Banco de México, S. A., México, D. F., 1954).

10 Madigan-Hyland Corporation, *The President Aleman Power Development and Markets for Papaloapan Power* (New York, 1951).

11 Alfonso Marquez L., "Informe del estudio agrológico detallado de una parte de la primera unidad agrícola del distrito de riego 'Presidente Miguel Alemán,' Veracruz" (Comisión del Papaloapan, 1951, unpublished).

12 Mexico, Sec. Econ., Dir. Gen. Estad., *Revista de estadística*, VIII, May 1945.

13 Mexico, Sec. Econ., Dir. Gen. Estad., *Septimo censo general de población. Resumen general* (1953).

14 Mexico, Sec. Econ., Dir. Gen. Estad., *Tercer censo agrícola ganadero y ejidal, 1950. Oaxaca* (1956).

15 Mexico, Sec. Econ., Dir. Gen. Estad., *Tercer censo agrícola ganadero y ejidal, 1950. Puebla* (1958).

16 Mexico, Sec. Econ., Dir. Gen. Estad., *Tercer censo agrícola ganadero y ejidal, 1950. Resumen general* (1956).

17 Mexico, Sec. Econ., Dir. Gen. Estad., *Tercer censo agrícola ganadero y ejidal, 1950. Veracruz* (1956).

18 Mexico, Sec. Fomento, Colonización e Industria, *Anuario estadístico de la república mexicana, 1903* (1905).

19 Mexico, Sec. Rec. Hid., Comisión del Papaloapan, *Compendio estadístico de la cuenca, 1960.*

20 F. A. Motz and L. D. Mallory, *The Fruit Industry of Mexico* (U.S. Dept. Agr., Off. For. Agr. Rel., For. Agr. Report No. 9, April 1944).

21 Armando Rodriguez Perales, *Introducción de forrajes en la cuenca del Papaloapan* (Comisión del Papaloapan, 1956).

22 Fernando Rosenzweig Hernandez, "Crédito agrícola en el Papaloapan," *El trimestre económico,* XXIV, April–June 1957.

23 Fernando Rosenzweig Hernandez, "El programa de crédito agrícola de la Comisión del Papaloapan" (Comisión del Papaloapan, March 1957, unpublished).

24 J. L. Tamayo, "El transporte ferrocarrilero en la cuenca del Papaloapan" (Comisión del Papaloapan, November 1954, unpublished).

25 *Tiempo* (México, D. F.), Feb. 4, 1957.

26 J. K. Turner, *Barbarous Mexico* (Chicago, 1911).

27 Alfonso Villa Rojas, *Los Mazatecos y el problema indigena de la cuenca del Papaloapan* (Memorias del Instituto Nacional Indigenista, vol. VII, México, D.F., 1955).

28 J. A. Vivó, *Geografía de México* (3d ed., México, D.F., and Buenos Aires, 1953).

29 W. W. Winnie, Jr., "The Lower Papaloapan Basin: Land and People" (diss., Univ. of Florida, 1956).

Chapter 5

THE PAPALOAPAN COMMISSION

The Papaloapan Project was conceived with the long-range objective of elevating per capita production in the basin through a variety of means. The development program, however, has clearly reflected the fact that the project grew out of the need to control the floods that periodically inundated much of the most productive land in the lower basin. In spite of interest in the region's broader potentialities, official concern with the area was almost exclusively on outgrowth of the flood problem, and the creation of the Papaloapan Commission in 1947 can be traced directly to an especially destructive deluge that occurred in late September 1944.

ORIGIN OF THE COMMISSION

The Flood Problem

There is every reason to believe that serious flooding in the lower basin has not been entirely a recent phenomenon. Archeological evidence suggests that repeated flooding forced at least one pre-Columbian tribe to abandon its lands along the river in favor of a more protected but less fertile location (5, p. 31). And a few decades after the Conquest, the mayor of the newly founded town of Tlacotalpan wrote, "When the [Papaloapan] river leaves its banks everything is flooded, and the corn and sweet-potato crops destroyed . . . and this is the usual situation in the majority of years" (quoted in 5, p. 31).

But destructive as these floods apparently were, they were less severe and less frequent than those that plagued the area during the present century. According to the Inter-Ministerial Commission appointed to investigate the flood of 1941:[1]

[1] Quotation from *Río Papaloapan: Problemas por desbordamiento de las aguas* (Informe rendido por la Comisión Intersecretarial de Agricultura, Comunicaciones y Marina, México, D.F., Dec. 18, 1943), as reproduced in *4*, part 1, p. 29.

89

All information is in agreement that the floods prior to 1921 were relatively infrequent and inundated the area for only three or four days, which in itself was beneficial to the land . . . After that date the floods occurred with greater frequency and each time [were] of longer duration. Thus, in 1931, 1935, and 1941, the settlements [along the rivers] were inundated for two or three months, with enormous losses to agriculture, and bringing about the danger that in time this fertile region would be converted into an unproductive wasteland.

There were apparently two reasons for this upturn in flooding. The Inter-Ministerial Commission suggested that a close correlation existed between flooding and the rapid rate of deforestation in some sections of the upper basin. The increased run-off and erosion, it was reasoned, were reflected in more and more siltation in the mature streams of the lower basin, so that progressively greater parts of a given high flow overtopped their banks and inundated the surrounding countryside. But in the view of José Noriega, whose study following the 1944 deluge was much more thorough, the increase resulted primarily from natural causes. He noted that the grade variations in the river system were in themselves highly conducive to erosion in the uplands and siltation in the coastal plain. The Santo Domingo, for instance, falls an average of 17.5 feet per mile during its course through the Sierra, whereas the Papaloapan drops less than .2 foot per mile as it flows to the sea. Consequently, the former has cut an ever-deepening gorge through the mountains, while so much silt has been deposited along the latter that its banks have become considerably higher than the surrounding flood-plain. This process, Noriega contended, was approaching a climax at just about the time when the effects of deforestation began to be felt. In his opinion, the *natural* rate of silting in the reaches near the foot of the Sierra had become so great that the Papaloapan was on the verge of a major, if geologically expected, change in course (*4*, part 1, pp. 31–32).

Whatever the principal cause, it is evident that the damage, severe to begin with, had grown progressively heavier. Although no detailed studies have been made to determine the extent of the area inundated by even the most recent floods, in the later years it was probably about 200,000 hectares. If the greater part of this area (whose general limits are shown in Map 9) was either unexploited or given over to seasonal pasture, it also included major segments of the sugar-cane and banana regions of the Papaloapan's flood-plain, the most heavily populated and most productive section of the lowlands.

Because most of the more serious floods took place during September and October (just before harvest time), they were particularly harmful to agriculture. Accurate assessment is impossible, but the Inter-Ministerial Commission estimated that the 1931 inundation destroyed roughly half of the lower basin's sugar-cane harvest and about a third of its banana plantings. Heavy losses were also sustained in livestock, either from drowning or from a more widespread incidence of disease after the flood. The Commission estimated that these three industries alone experiencd losses in the neighborhood of 6.5 million pesos ($3.25 million at the rate of exchange then prevailing) (*4*, part 1, p. 34; part 2, p. 38).

Taking these data as a reference point and reckoning that destruction was at least 50 per cent greater than in 1931, Noriega calculated the total direct losses caused by the 1944 deluge at 30 million pesos, broken down as follows (*4*, part 1, pp. 34–39):

Category	Million pesos
Agricultural products	11.0
Livestock	.7
Urban property	8.0
Communications	6.0
Wages lost	4.0

Large as this total is, it probably represents a substantial underestimate. Noriega not only failed to consider agricultural losses other than to sugar cane and bananas but also neglected to make full allowance for the decline in the value of the peso after 1931.

Periodic damage to property was not the only serious consequence of the flood problem. Over 100 lives were reported lost in the 1944 inundation, and countless other persons were stricken by diseases fostered by the unsanitary conditions left by high water.

Moreover, there is evidence that the tempo of development in the lowlands fell off markedly, at least after 1940, as an outgrowth of repeated inundations. The fact that the population of the important sugar-producing municipality of Cosamaloapan (on the western margin of the Papaloapan near the town of the same name) increased by only 20 per cent between 1940 and 1950 (when demand conditions in the world and domestic sugar markets were excellent) as opposed to more than 50 per cent during the previous decade (when far less favorable conditions prevailed) has been attributed entirely to the disrupted communications and property losses occasioned by the floods (2, p. 15).

Governmental Involvement

The federal government's concern with the flood problem dates from the inundation of 1941. In response to an appeal from the town of Cosamaloapan, an Inter-Ministerial Commission was created in 1943. It was composed of representatives from the Ministries of Communications, Agriculture, and the Navy, and charged with gathering information that could prepare the way for positive assistance. The Commission's report, completed in less than two months, concluded that both flood-control works in the lowlands and an extensive program of reforestation in the upper basin were necessary, and that the situation had become critical enough to warrant the initiation of both on a crash basis (5, p. 33). But because of the magnitude of the investment that would have been involved these recommendations were ignored, and none of the three ministries continued an active interest in the area.

In late September 1944, a particularly powerful hurricane dumped torrents of water on much of southeastern Mexico, and left in its wake the most destructive flood ever recorded in the basin. The damage and suffering wrought by this deluge shocked the entire country and moved President Avila Camacho to visit the region. As a result of this inspection, a further survey was ordered, not only to point the way to protective works, but to suggest means for promoting economic growth throughout the basin.

This task was assigned to the National Irrigation Commission

(Comisión Nacional de Irrigación), the agency which since 1926 had been responsible for the federal land reclamation program— mostly irrigation projects in the northern part of the country. The Commission, in turn, hired a group of engineers headed by José Noriega to make the study. Their report was submitted in June 1946.

The findings of this group indicated to Noriega that "a solution [was] not only possible but relatively simple" (4, part 1, p. 8). Although he concluded that this solution could not be set forth in its final form until after considerably more information about the basin's hydrology had become available, he suggested that it would probably take the form of a number of dams on the Papaloapan's tributaries. As to immediate works, he indicated that construction of one of these dams, together with a series of levees and a by-pass canal, would be sufficient initially to protect the most important of the flooded areas, the heavily populated margins of the Papaloapan.

But he also pointed out that (4, part 1, p. 6)

control of the Papaloapan and the general development of the region cannot be achieved without an enormous expenditure of money and effort—probably superior to [the total expended] by the National Irrigation Commission in the 20 years [of its existence]. . . . The hydraulic works as such will not [necessitate such an investment], but the unhealthiness and isolation of the region complicate any important works of investigation or construction. . . . These two factors constitute much more of a stumbling block than the serious technical and financial difficulties involved.

To undertake the numerous detailed investigations prerequisite to the formulation of a comprehensive development plan and to begin construction of the various immediate flood-control and access facilities, Noriega recommended the creation of an organization differing distinctly from the other dependencies of the National Irrigation Commission. Because the proposed project would have a scope far broader than that of any previously attempted by the Commission and would deal with a (tropical) region in which that body's earlier experience would be of little relevance, a degree of administrative automony was suggested. This proposal was adopted by President Alemán shortly thereafter. A native of the lower basin, Alemán had included among his campaign promises a pledge to initiate a program of regional development in the Papaloapan basin. This promise was fulfilled when, in February 1947, he created the Papaloapan Commission.

THE COMMISSION AS AN AGENCY FOR ECONOMIC DEVELOPMENT

The creation of the Papaloapan Commission marked two important milestones in the course of governmental efforts to hasten Mexico's economic growth. We have noted that the Papaloapan Project was the first major project to be concerned with the humid tropics. The organizational form of the Commission was also significant. As the country's first experiment with the regional approach to development, it marked the beginning of a second major trend; within five years of its creation, three other such agencies had been formed, all of them patterned after the Commission.[2]

The Commission has been referred to as "Mexico's TVA" (cf. 5, p. 41). To a degree, the implied comparison is justified. Both the Tennessee Valley Authority and the Commission were products of precedent-making decisions by their respective federal governments to set up developmental authorities for an entire river basin. And both were motivated in the main by flood-control objectives. But beyond that the similarity is tenuous. Unlike the TVA, which enjoys a completely autonomous position in what political scientists like to call the "headless fourth branch of government," the Commission has exercised only partial autonomy and falls entirely within the jurisdiction of the federal executive.

The legal basis of the Commission rests in an executive decree issued by President Alemán on February 26, 1947.[3] According to

---

[2] The three: the *Comisión del Tepalcatepec* (1947), the *Comisión del Río Fuerte* (1951), and the *Comisión del Grijalva* (1951). In 1960 the Comisión del Tepalcatepec was absorbed into the new *Comisión del Río Balsas*.

[3] The Commission's status was confirmed by legislation on December 27, 1951.

the brief and none-too-informative phraseology of this decree, the Commission was constituted as a federal agency "to formulate, plan, and construct the works necessary for the integral development of that portion of the country which makes up the basin of the Papaloapan River." To this end, it was granted "full authority to plan . . . and construct all works for flood control, irrigation, power generation, communication—including water transport, ports, roads, railroads, telegraphs, and telephones—and urbanization" in the area, and was also endowed with "full powers to dictate the . . . disposition of industrial, agricultural, and colonization matters insofar as they pertain to the [region's] integral development" (3, p, 181).

What this sweeping mandate has meant in terms of actual power has depended largely on the attitude of the three national administrations that have directed the Commission's activities. Generally speaking, however, it has been interpreted as giving the Commission a type of dual authority, one over a development program of its own, the second in connection with the activities of other government agencies. With respect to the former, the authority originally granted was both broad and complete; at its outset and for about ten years thereafter, the Commission enjoyed full powers for planning and executing a comprehensive program of regional development. But in connection with the activities of other agencies, its authority has always been quite limited. The Commission was never intended to replace completely the other executive bodies operating in the basin. These agencies have in the final analysis retained all their rights and duties, the Commission having simply been added to the existing governmental framework. But to provide a basis for inter-agency cooperation and planning, the Commission has played the role of coordinator. As with the Tennessee Valley Authority in the United States, however, this role was not accompanied by powers of enforcement (1, p. 9). Outside its own direct works, the Commission can argue and entreat, but it has been able to command only voluntary cooperation.

The Commission is a dependency of the National Irrigation Commission's successor agency, the Ministry of Hydraulic Resources

(Secretaría de Recursos Hidraulicos).[4] Its budgetary appropriations are received through that body, and the Ministry's policy-making officials keep its activities under continual review. Nonetheless, it differed markedly with regard to both its scope of activity and its organizational make-up from any dependency that either the Irrigation Commission or the Ministry had previously directed. Instead of being concerned with a single phase of development, irrigation, like the earlier operating agencies, the Commission was, in effect, created to carry on the wide range of functions for which, had they chosen collectively to encourage development in the Papaloapan basin, a number of federal ministries would have been responsible. Therefore, rather than being made wholly subordinate to only one ministry, it was granted a measure of autonomy.

The extent of this autonomy and the manner in which it was initially intended to be exercised are best explained with reference to Chart 7, which is a simplified diagram of the Commission's internal organization and its relationship to the federal bureaucracy as of 1956, the year in which the Commission reached perhaps the zenith of its power. The Commission itself is composed of three members: the Minister of Hydraulic Resources, who acts as its president, a *Vocal Ejecutivo*, and a *Vocal Secretario*, all of whom are appointed by the President of the Republic and serve at his pleasure.[5] The Minister is the agency's titular chief, but in practice the Vocal Ejecutivo acts as its operating head and the Vocal Secretario as his first deputy.

This diagram illustrates the Commission's twofold responsibility: a primary one to the Ministry of Hydraulic Resources, and a secondary one to the other ministries whose functions are included within its mandate. As to the first of these, the Vocal Ejecutivo is the direct representative of the Minister of Hydraulic Resources and is accountable to him for all the Commission's activities. At the same time, however, both he and the Vocal Secretario enjoy the au-

---

[4] The National Irrigation Commission, a dependency of the Ministry of Agriculture, was elevated to ministerial status in December 1946.

[5] The terms Vocal Ejecutivo and Vocal Secretario do not lend themselves to precise translation. Literally, a vocal is one empowered to speak for an organization, much as the president of a corporation speaks for it. Perhaps the most meaningful translation would be "Executive Director" and "Executive Secretary."

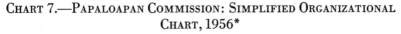

CHART 7.—PAPALOAPAN COMMISSION: SIMPLIFIED ORGANIZATIONAL
CHART, 1956*

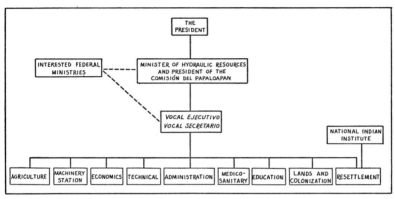

*Adapted from "Cuadro general de organización, 1956" (Comisión del Papaloapan, January 1956, unpublished).

thority to deal directly with any other ministry whose functions the Commission's activities may touch upon. For instance, the Commission's road-building program has been shaped and executed in close cooperation with the Ministry of Communications. Herein lies the essence of the Commission's semi-autonomous character: as other ministries may bring pressure to bear on the Vocales, so the Vocales have the authority to deal directly with them. The resulting give-and-take has produced an organization that is somewhat independent of its parent.

In practice, the powers and authority of the Commission have varied considerably. During the six years of the Alemán administration the project was decidedly in official favor—it was thought, in fact, that Alemán would become its Vocal Ejecutivo after leaving the the Presidency—and the Commission enjoyed a good deal of true autonomy. Budgetary limitations were minimal, and since few of the other executive branches had much interest in what was happening in the basin, they were not disposed to interfere. But once the project became established and (starting in about 1952) began to branch out from strictly flood-control and access works, they grew increasingly worried. The Commission was now heavily involved in activities that had once been their exclusive domain, and this smacked of "empire building" on the part of the Ministry of Hydraulic Resources. Late 1956 was the turning point. At that time the Commission was deprived of a particularly forceful Vocal Ejecutivo through an airplane accident, and as the result of a series of high-level decisions its activities and budget were sharply curtailed. It has been on the defensive ever since.

CITATIONS

1 Gordon R. Clapp, "The Meaning of TVA," in Roscoe C. Martin, ed., *TVA: The First Twenty Years* (Presses of the Universities of Alabama and Tennessee, 1956).

2 Madigan-Hyland Corporation, *The President Aleman Power Development and Markets for Papaloapan Power* (New York, 1951).

3 Mexico, Sec. Rec. Hid., Comisión del Papaloapan, *Economía del Papaloapan: Evaluación de las inversiones y sus efectos* (1958).

4 J. S. Noriega, "Control del río Papaloapan: Preparación del plan de estudios definitivos y programa de construcción de las obras," *Ingenieria hidráulica en México*, I, April–June 1947 (part 1); and *ibid.*, I, July–September 1947 (part 2).

5 Alfonso Villa Rojas, *El Papaloapan: Obra del presidente Alemán, 1947–1952* (Comisión del Papaloapan, 1952).

Chapter 6

DEVELOPMENT OBJECTIVES AND THE RECORD OF ACCOMPLISHMENT

The 16 years of the Papaloapan Project have brought about important changes in the Papaloapan basin and its economy. These have been particularly pronounced in the lower basin. The fertile lands along the Papaloapan have been largely freed of the danger of flooding, and, thanks to a new system of roads, substantial new tracts have been opened to agriculture. In the uplands, too, a noteworthy beginning has been made. Several new roads have been pushed into the hinterland of the upper basin, and for the first time, the people there are learning of the world beyond their own villages.

If this suggests that the lower basin at least is now well on the way to sustained economic growth, it does not follow that the project has been completely successful. Nor does it follow that the Commission's activities have been based on the logical unfolding of a preconceived plan of development. Instead, much of the program has evolved through trial and error, and on several occasions it has undergone major alterations in order to conform with changing national policies. The result has been a number of abandoned schemes, failures, and expensive errors.

PLANNING PROBLEMS

Given the conditions under which the Commission was created, a preconceived plan of development could hardly have been expected. At the time the project was begun in 1947, neither the basin's natural attributes nor the socio-economic characteristics of its population were well understood. Information about the area's hydrology, essential to a sound program of flood control, was almost totally absent; and little was known about its actual economy, let alone about the type, extent, and capabilities of its potentially productive resources. The existing surveys of the basin, those undertaken by the Inter-Ministerial Commission and by Noriega's group, had been prepared after only a few months of study, and were necessarily quite superficial. Their value lay more in their usefulness as guideposts for further investigation than as the bases for detailed pre-planning.

In the circumstances, the ideal procedure would have been to postpone all major programs until after the basin had been studied in detail and a fairly comprehensive plan drawn up. The long delay inherent here, however, was considered inconsistent with the principal reason for the Commission's creation, the desire to give the more populated sections of the lowlands an immediate measure of flood protection. Since this goal could not be achieved without involving many works whose ramifications would be more general (e.g., roads and the like), the authorities had little choice but to compromise. They were, in effect, forced to begin a program of development while still in the process of collecting and interpreting the necessary basic evidence.

If this fact goes far toward defining the planning problems the Commission has experienced, a second element has led to no fewer difficulties. This has been that each of the three national administrations under which the Commission has operated has followed its own approach to economic development, and has had its own views on the scope of the project, the size of its budget, and the functions for which the Commission should be responsible. The resulting conflicts have been major ones. Thus, the changeover from President Alemán (1946–52) to President Ruiz Cortines (1952–58) saw the nature of the project basically altered. And in 1957 and again in 1959, similarly drastic revisions were necessary.

INITIAL AND REVISED OBJECTIVES

Phase 1 (1947–1952)

In May 1947, the broad objectives of the project were set forth by Adolfo Orive Alba, Minister of Hydraulic Resources and President of the Commission during the Alemán administration, as follows (*10,* pp. 41–42):

1. Control of the rivers to prevent serious flooding in the lower basin.
2. Conversion of the basin into a healthful place in which to live.
3. Promotion of agriculuture through drainage and supplemental-irrigation schemes.
4. Generation of electric power to encourage industrialization in the basin and neighboring regions.
5. Creation of new urban centers and the improvement of existing ones.
6. Conversion of the river system into a good navigable waterway.
7. Construction of an adequate communications network.

However, few specific goals were formalized at that time, or for that matter during the first six years of the project. Rather, the Commission's authorities seem to have set out initially to follow the broad recommendations of Noriega's group while gathering the information needed for more detailed planning.

The guideposts established by Noriega dealt almost entirely with the flood problem. In the most general terms, he suggested that the key to this problem and the over-all development of the basin probably lay in the construction of five multi-purpose dams and their associated facilities.[1] These dams, he felt, could be designed not only to reduce the peak flows of the various rivers, but also to generate power, to divert water for irrigation, and to regulate the flow of water into the lower basin in a way that would render its rivers more navigable.

Although Noriega cautioned that much more information would be needed before this or any other broad approach could be accepted with confidence, he was fairly specific in his recommendations for immediate works. To bring a prompt measure of protection from flooding to the productive lands along the Papaloapan, he suggested that certain defense and control works for that region—including

---

[1] See map in *8,* part 1, p. 12, for the proposed location of these dams.

TABLE 9.—PAPALOAPAN COMMISSION: COMPOSITION OF
EXPENDITURES, 1947–1960*

(Per cent)

Category	1947–52	1953–56	1957–58	1959–60	Total
Communications	23	25	52	31	30
Flood control	46	25	6	14	26
Agriculture	3	22	5	5	12
Others	28	28	37	50	32
Total expenditures *(million 1954 pesos)* ..	329.9	385.3	151.1	48.8	915.1

* Calculated from Table 10.

levees, a by-pass canal, and one major dam near where the Tonto and
Santo Domingo meet to form the Papaloapan—be expedited. And
since the probable sites for these and the likely future projects were
generally accessible only by small boat or horseback, he advised early
commencement of a road-building program (*8*, part 2, pp. 30–31).

These recommendations were closely reflected in the composition
of the Commission's expenditures during the six years of the Alemán
administration (Tables 9 and 10). Almost half of its outlays during
this period went into various flood-control works, the most important
being the huge Alemán Dam.[2] This dam, one of the largest in Latin
America, controls the Tonto, in terms of flow the most significant of
the Papaloapan's tributaries. Of the remaining expenditure, about
half was allocated to the construction of access roads in the lower
basin. The greater part of this outlay was invested in two highways:
one from Tinajas to Ciudad Alemán, connecting the heart of the lowlands and the center of the Commission's activities with the Mexico
City–Veracruz highway; the other, built atop a new levee protecting
the western margin of the Papaloapan, running from Ciudad Alemán
to Tlacotalpan. In addition to these major projects, sanitary engineering and educational programs were initiated, primarily in those
parts of the coastal plain neighboring on the Commission's chief

[2] The locations of the Commission's various projects are shown in Map 10.

works; and various urban improvement schemes, particularly the construction of the Commission's headquarters town, Ciudad Alemán, were carried out. But these secondary activities were of comparatively minor importance; over two-thirds of the budget was expended on the Alemán Dam and the two main highways.

The similarity between Noriega's suggestions and the Commission's early projects does not mean, however, that all his recommendations were put into effect. An appraisal of the extent of fundamental knowledge about the basin as of early 1953 clearly indicates that during the project's first six years insufficient attention was given to the basic studies recommended by Noriega. Indeed, the officials who took over the project in December 1952 complained that during the latter part of the Alemán administration basic studies were virtually suspended, while full attention was focused on the immediate works that had been initiated (2, p. 3). And it is also clear that many of the projects were carried out not as suggested but in a manner which, given the basin's stage of development, must be regarded as ill-conceived and grandiose.

Thus, the Tinajas–Ciudad Alemán road was constructed as a magnificent three-lane, well-graded, and almost curveless paved highway despite the fact that it traversed an area otherwise devoid of all-weather roads; the Alemán Dam was designed partly for irrigation purposes before any studies indicating the desirability of supplemental irrigation in the lower basin were conducted; and Ciudad Alemán was laid out for an eventual 150,000 inhabitants (10, p. 59), although several well-established towns were situated nearby. On the basis of these considerations alone, one can only conclude that during its first six years the Papaloapan Project contained characteristics of the proverbial *proyectismo* of Latin America.

Phase 2 (1953–1956)

The public investment policy of Adolfo Ruiz Cortines, who succeeded Alemán as President in December 1952, differed sharply from that of his predecessors. Following consolidation of the Revolution during the 1920's, successive federal administrations had at-

TABLE 10.—PAPALOAPAN COMMISSION: EXPENDITURES BY MAJOR CATEGORY, 1947–1960*

(*Million pesos*)

Category	1947-52[a]	1953	1954	1955	1956	1957	1958	1959	1960	Total
Communications	62.7[b]	8.9	19.7	31.8	38.8	48.6	52.4	14.9	5.3	283.1
Flood Control........	124.5	63.3	27.5	6.8	3.2	2.4	9.2	6.6	2.2	245.8
Alemán Dam	118.6	52.7	20.4	4.5	2.1	1.1	6.4	4.1	.5	210.4
Other works[c]	5.9	10.6	7.2	2.3	1.2	1.3	2.9	2.5	1.7	35.4
Agriculture	8.5	23.2	24.8	24.9	13.6	6.1	2.7	1.4	2.0	107.2
Experiments, credit, tech. assistance ...	5.6	2.7	2.7	7.6	7.4	3.8	1.8	1.4	2.0	35.1
Río Blanco irrigation.	—	18.8	18.3	13.7	5.8	2.3	.6	—	—	59.6
Los Naranjos irrigation	—	1.4	3.2	3.2	.4	—	—	—	—	8.2
Michapan irrigation..	2.9	.1	.7	.4	—	—	.2	—	—	4.2
Others..............	76.1	19.8	27.6	33.2	33.2	31.9	38.5	18.0	14.8	293.2
Sanitary engineering[d]	15.6	2.4	2.6	4.5	4.4	2.8	4.0	2.8	2.5	41.7
Resettlement[e]	.7	5.4	4.6	4.5	5.8	6.7	6.6	1.1	2.6	38.0
Studies	7.8	1.6	2.5	3.4	3.6	2.6	4.9	2.3	2.2	30.9
School construction and education	3.8	.6	1.4	2.5	3.8	3.8	5.6	2.5	2.0	26.4

Others (*continued*)

Urban improvement	13.0	.5	2.0	3.0	.5	.8	1.6	.2	.1	21.8
Administration	17.4	6.4	7.6	6.8	7.7	8.0	9.7	7.7	5.2	76.6
Equipment and miscellaneous	17.7	2.8	6.9	8.2	7.5	7.2	6.2	1.4	.2	57.9
Total	**271.9**	**115.1**	**99.7**	**96.6**	**88.9**	**89.0**	**102.8**	**40.8**	**24.3**	**929.2**
Total in 1954 pesos[f]	329.9	125.9	99.7	85.0	74.7	71.8	79.3	31.1	17.7	915.1

* Data for 1947–58 from Mexico, Sec. Rec. Hid., Comisión del Papaloapan, *Breves apuntes acerca de la cuenca del Papaloapan y de la labor realizada por la Comisión* (1959), Table 10; for 1959–60 from "Planificación integral de la cuenca del Papaloapan" (paper presented at the 5th National Congress of Civil Engineering, Veracruz, October 1961), p. 23. Because of rounding, numbers will not necessarily add to totals.

[a] Yearly expenditures in 1947–52 were (in million pesos): 1947—7.8; 1948 — 16.0; 1949 — 21.0; 1950 — 37.5; 1951 — 77.9; 1952 — 111.6.

[b] Includes the entire 21 million peso cost of the Ciudad Alemán–Tlacotalpan highway. Because this highway is built on a levee, an unknown portion of its cost should more properly be charged to flood control.

[c] Includes levees and rectification cuts, but not the cost of the levee on the west bank of the Papaloapan.

[d] Chiefly sanitary drinking water systems, but also direct medical assistance.

[e] Resettlement of persons displaced by the reservoir of the Alemán Dam.

[f] Annual expenditures adjusted by the index of wholesale prices for 210 articles in Mexico City computed by the Banco de México, S. A.

tempted to stimulate Mexico's development, chiefly through building up the economy's infrastructure—roads, schools, irrigation facilities, and similar social overheads. This was particularly true of the Avila Camacho (1940–46) and Alemán regimes. And, as we have noted, so it was with the Commission during Alemán's term of office.

In the initial stages of development, the principal need for public investment is most often in the realm of social overheads; without adequate provision of an economic infrastructure, general progress can hardly be begun, much less sustained. But a governmental program oriented almost exclusively along such lines need not yield maximum returns, especially with regard to agricultural production. In a basically capitalistic society, improved overhead facilities may stimulate individual entrepreneurs in other sectors of the economy to expand output, but where agriculture is both backward and dominated by smallholders, as in Mexico, the agrarian sector may be comparatively slow to respond. Unless additional services—credit, technical advice, and other forms of direct assistance—are made available, the peasant's limited capital resources and technical knowledge usually prevent his taking full advantage of the improved infrastructure.

There is evidence that precisely this happened in Mexico during the Avila Camacho and Alemán administrations. Under both regimes overhead works were stressed almost to the exclusion of complementary measures; and under both, according to the findings of the Combined Mexican Working Party, the results of the federal land reclamation program, for one, fell well short of what might otherwise have been expected (*4*, p. 26).

All this changed when Ruiz Cortines took office. Instead of continuing to emphasize overhead works, he and his advisors determined to give greater attention to the more direct forms of assistance. Whether this shift was motivated by an appreciation of the previous lack of balance, a desire to reduce the costs of governmental activities while at the same time spreading the effects more widely among the agrarian population, or merely to place greater weight on immediate rather than future returns has never been fully clarified. The effect, in any event, was to compel the new group of officials who took charge of the Commission in December 1952 to alter its goals markedly.

In many respects, this ushered in the most exciting period of the Papaloapan Project. Money continued to be comparatively abundant, and during the first four years of the Ruiz Cortines administration the Commission enjoyed the leadership of a Vocal Ejecutivo who was uncommonly capable and not afraid to experiment. In place of the construction of a few major flood-control and access facilities in the lowlands, he attempted to stress a wider variety of less spectacular means to stimulate development throughout the entire basin. Almost contemptuous of the super-highways already built, he immediately laid plans for a secondary and feeder road system in both the lower basin and the hitherto isolated highlands; and renewed efforts were made to determine how the Commission's contribution might most effectively be exerted. Direct aid to agriculture received greater emphasis. Several colonization schemes were started, as was a new program of agricultural credit.

During these years the first specific plan for the project began to take shape, and given time a reasonably balanced program would no doubt have evolved. As tentatively outlined in late 1955 in a report to the Investments Committee of the President's Office (2), this revised plan looked to the achievement of two broad goals. One was to open to more intensive exploitation substantial portions of the virgin or extensively utilized lands in the basin's tropical sections. The other was to spread more widely the beneficial effects of the Commission's educational and sanitary engineering operations. Flood control, drainage, and irrigation schemes were sharply downgraded.

As to the first of these objectives, the agricultural potentialities of the basin were taken rather as a matter of faith. Even as this is written, a truly detailed survey of the area's land resources remains to be taken. But underlying the creation of the Commission as a multi-purpose development agency was the assumption that most of the sparsely settled tropical portions are potentially far more productive than past utilization would indicate. Specifically, it has been assumed that, except for some 200,000 hectares of low-lying terrain near the Laguna de Alvarado which would require either drainage or flood-control works prior to reclamation, almost the entire uncultivated portion of the coastal plain—roughly 1.2 million hectares—is capable of supporting crop agriculture or at least a more intensive type of livestock production. And of an estimated 1.3 million hectares in the tropical sections of the Sierra's windward slope, it has been assumed that at least 300,000–400,000 hectares in the lower reaches, particularly in the virtually uninhabited region southeast of Valle Nacional, have a sufficiently gentle slope to warrant cropping or livestock enterprises (2, pp. 7–8; 9, p. 7).

Of these areas, the 1955 plan called for the Commission to actively promote the development of 300,000 hectares in the lowlands and 130,000 hectares in the windward slope. The approach was to be a coordinated one. As new roads were built, colonists were to be brought in, and they and the local residents were to be given credits and technical guidance by the Commission. The proposed target date was 1970. It was suggested that in that year, with the new lands under exploitation and the accelerated development of the basin presumably well under way, the Commission should be dissolved and its activities turned over to the interested federal ministries and private initiative.

Since this tentative plan evolved gradually as the Commission's new officials came to terms with their responsibilities, it did not greatly affect the pattern of the Commission's expenditures until about 1955. Until then, completion of the various works begun during the first six years, notably the Alemán Dam, continued to absorb the greater part of the budget. Nor did the plan really have a chance to get beyond the pilot project stage thereafter. For in November 1956 a tragic airplane crash took the life of Raúl Sandoval Landázuri, the Commission's young and vigorous Vocal Ejecutivo, and with him perished much of the new life with which the project had been infused.

Phase 3 (1957–1958)

The death of Ing. Sandoval marked a watershed in the evolution of the Papaloapan Project. During its first decade the Commission gradually developed into a truly multi-purpose agency, until by 1956 it was involved in such diverse functions as colonization, agricultural credit, and school construction, not to mention its flood-control and communications programs. Since then the pendulum has swung in the opposite direction. One after another, the Commission has been forced to terminate or to curtail its peripheral activities drastically and to concentrate more and more on road construction and the development of water resources.

If the precise decisions and bureaucratic compromises that led to this turn of events are obscure, their cause is clear. As the Commission branched out into fields that had previously been the exclusive territory of other federal agencies, their administrators understandably became concerned that the Ministry of Hydraulic Resources, through the Commission, was expanding at their expense. With the death of the Commission's Vocal Ejecutivo and the subsequent review of instructions to his successor, these individuals were afforded an excellent opportunity to bring pressure for a change. For their interests the outcome was both favorable and sweeping. In early 1957 the Commission's agricultural stations were transferred to the Ministry of Agriculture, and many of its medico-sanitary operations to the Ministry of Public Health; and its credit and colonization operations were curtailed. During the remaining two years of the Ruiz Cortines administration, the Commission functioned mainly as a road-building agency; over half its budget was allocated to that end.

Phase 4 (1959–)

The setback suffered in 1957 was prolonged, and was in fact heightened after President López Mateos took office in December 1958. Unlike his predecessors, López Mateos has shown no particular interest in the project, and as Tables 9 and 10 show, his administration has been marked by drastic curtailments in the Commission's budget.[3] In effect, the project has been in abeyance since 1961, with virtually all new investment suspended and most of the limited supply of funds going for the maintenance of works long since completed.

[3] The Commission was allegedly involved in certain personal and budgetary irregularities during the closing years of the Ruiz Cortines administration. This may in part account for López Mateos' attitude.

With this has come a sharp cut in staff; whereas in 1956 the Commission employed upwards of 1,500 persons (about equally divided between laborers and technical and administrative personnel), in 1961 it could count only a third as many. Still, much remains to be done, and though the immediate outlook for the project is problematical, planning continues against the time that funds will once again be available; 1976 or thereabouts is now viewed as the logical completion date.

THE RECORD OF ACCOMPLISHMENT

Despite the unusual number of planning and budgetary difficulties it has encountered, the Commission can look back on a creditable record of achievement, especially in its communications and flood-control programs. And if its other efforts have on the whole been less fruitful, as in the case of its agricultural activities, a valuable backlog of experience with the problems of stimulating development in tropical areas has been accumulated.

Communications

In terms of both results achieved and money expended (through 1960 it accounted for 30 per cent of the project's budget), the most significant of the Commission's works has been its communications program. This program has been essentially one of road building.[4] Although authority was granted to improve and extend the rail system, no additions have been made. A shortage of rolling-stock and poor maintenance of stationary facilities, rather than insufficient trackage, have been regarded as the principal deficiencies of the basin's railroads. Since similar conditions characterize most of the country's rail network, the solution has been regarded as lying in national rather than regional rehabilitation programs.

So too with the river system; although one of the Commission's initial goals was to improve the navigability of the river system, this

---

[4] A program of airfield construction, most of it in the highlands, has also been undertaken. But the objectives have been very limited, and the 34 small fields thus far built have been useful mainly in opening up the least accessible portions of the basin to survey groups, medical technicians, and the like.

objective has not really been pursued as such. Studies in 1954 revealed that in order to rehabilitate the river network an investment of about 100 million pesos in addition to the outlays budgeted for flood control would be required, and that the areas which would be affected could be reached more economically by roads (*1*, p. 83). Nevertheless, some of the works designed primarily for flood control have improved the Papaloapan's navigability, and future structures may be expected similarly to benefit the other navigable streams.

A comparison of Maps 9 and 10 indicates the number of roads that have been built. In 1947 there were only about 125 miles of highway in the basin. By 1961 the network, including roads partially completed but passable, had been extended to over 1,500 miles. With the exception of one or two comparatively minor regions, the agricultural centers of the tierra caliente are now served by road, and a significant beginning has been made toward overcoming the isolation of the upper basin.

However, not all of this increase can be attributed to the Commission. The national highway network of the Ministry of Communications now accounts for about 250 miles of roadway within the basin, and can be thought of as roughly circumscribing the area. And the National Committee for Farm-to-Market Roads has completed several important feeder roads in the upper basin. But the Commission, either directly or in cooperation with other government or private groups, is responsible for over three-quarters of the present system.

In spite of the inevitable waste growing out of some duplication of facilities, the experience of several localities now served both by road and by rail or water transportation indicates that the Commission's emphasis on roads has been entirely justifiable. Because of the greater speed and flexibility of truck service, road transportation knows no peer in a developing area of smallholder agriculture. For example, between 1941 and 1946 the freight carried by the Alvarado-Veracruz railroad increased by about a quarter. In 1947 the road paralleling this line was rebuilt as an all-weather highway, and by 1948, despite the fact that truck rates were almost double those of the trains, truck competition had reduced rail freight by 40 per cent

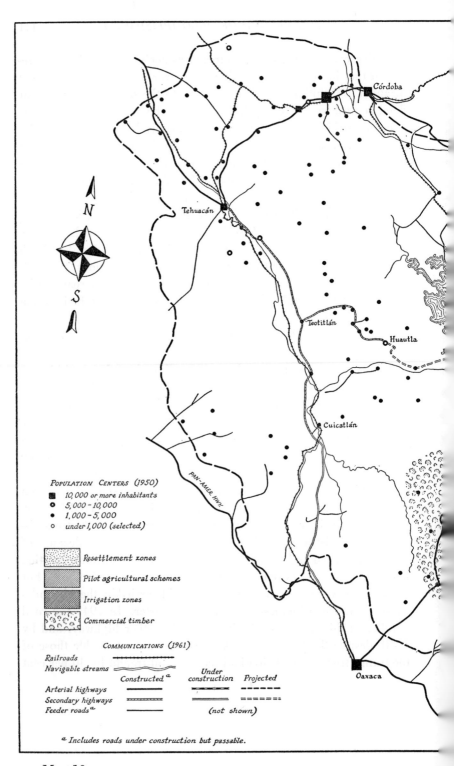

POPULATION CENTERS (1950)

- 10,000 or more inhabitants
- 5,000 – 10,000
- 1,000 – 5,000
- under 1,000 (selected)

Resettlement zones

Pilot agricultural schemes

Irrigation zones

Commercial timber

COMMUNICATIONS (1961)

Railroads
Navigable streams

	Constructed ᵃ	Under construction	Projected
Arterial highways			
Secondary highways			
Feeder roads ᵃ		(not shown)	

ᵃ Includes roads under construction but passable.

MAP 10

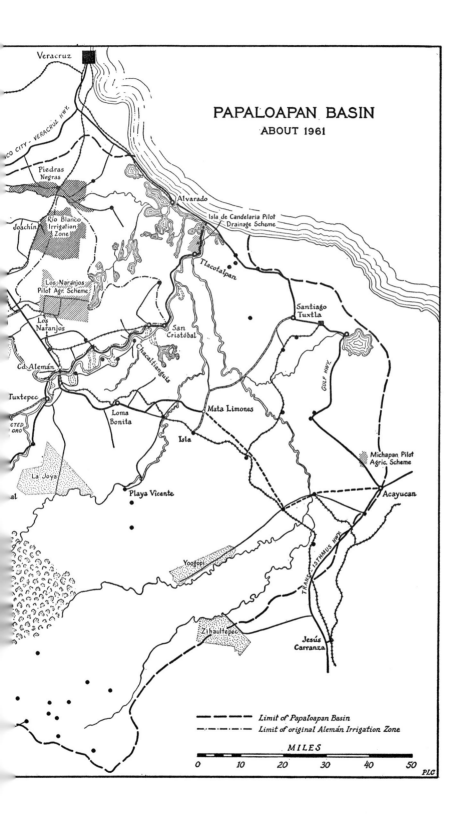

PAPALOAPAN BASIN
ABOUT 1961

Veracruz

CO CITY - VERACRUZ HWY.

Piedras
Negras

Río Blanco
Irrigation
Zone

Joachín

Alvarado

Isla de Candelaria Pilot
Drainage Scheme

Tlacotalpan

Los Naranjos
Pilot Agr. Scheme

Los
Naranjos

San
Cristóbal

Santiago
Tuxtla

Cd. Alemán

Chacaltianguis

Tuxtepec

CTED
ORO

Loma
Bonita

Mata Limones

GULF HWY.

Isla

Michapan Pilot
Agric. Scheme

La Joya

Playa Vicente

Acayucan

al

Yoogopi

TRANS-ISTHMUS HWY.

Zihaultepec

Jesús
Carranza

Limit of Papaloapan Basin
Limit of original Alemán Irrigation Zone

MILES

0   10   20   30   40   50

PLC

of the 1946 volume (*4*, pp. 92, 316). Prior to 1955, communication between Tuxtepec and Valle Nacional was confined to the rivers. When in that year an all-weather road joined the two points, river traffic ceased to exist. Motor transport resulted not only in a drastic reduction in hauling time (from one and one-half days to three hours) and a significant lowering of rates (by 22 per cent) but in far better treatment of merchandise (*1*, pp. 8–9).

As for the future, it is hoped that by 1976 (or whenever the project is completed) the road network will have been increased to some 3,000 miles, or about doubled. As is true of most of the mileage today, the bulk of this system is scheduled for gravel surfacing.[5] But it is expected that by then traffic on most of the arterial and secondary highways will be heavy enough to warrant paving.

Flood Control

The Commission's flood-control program, the original *raison d'être* for the Papaloapan Project, has removed the threat of serious flooding in the main agricultural and population centers along the rivers of the lower basin. The entire western margin of the Papaloapan (as far north as Tlacotalpan), where the greatest losses were previously suffered, now enjoys adequate protection, as do the more heavily populated sections along the river's eastern bank. Only in areas with a comparatively small number of people and a limited agricultural base—the Papaloapan's eastern margin north of Chacaltianguis and the lower reaches of the Tesechoacan and San Juan rivers—is periodic flooding still a threat.

The Alemán Dam is chiefly responsible for this improvement. Over 1.8 miles in length and rising 250 feet above the river bed, this vast earth-filled structure controls the Tonto, the tributary that (because of its course through the high rainfall area along the base of the Sierra Madre) is responsible for the largest share of the water flowing into the Papaloapan. The dam has been far and away the

[5] Apart from the highways built by the Ministry of Communications (the Mexico City–Veracruz, the Gulf, and the Trans-Isthmus highways) only the roads between Tinajas and Ciudad Alemán and between Ciudad Alemán and Tlacotalpan are now paved.

Commission's most expensive single venture. Of the quarter of its outlays that has gone for flood control, 85 per cent has been invested in the dam; and through 1954, when the dam was completed, it accounted for fully 40 per cent of the project's entire budget.

A number of complementary flood-control works have also been completed. Seven rectification cuts have substantially augmented the discharge capacity of the Papaloapan by speeding its flow and by reducing (by about a quarter) the flowing distance between Tuxtepec and Alvarado. Levees totaling over 100 miles protect the river's western margin from Tuxtepec to Tlacotalpan and the eastern bank as far north as Chacaltianguis. And a floodway has been built to permit a portion of the river's peak flows to be diverted directly into the Laguna de Alvarado. Together, these works have reduced the area subject to flooding from around 200,000 hectares to about half that much.

The reservoir created by the Alemán Dam has a capacity of over 8,000 million cubic meters and covers almost 50,000 hectares. This area was once the home of some 22,000 Mazatec Indians, and the flood-control effort has led to a large resettlement operation. This difficult operation has for the most part been handled for the Commission by the National Indian Institute (Instituto Nacional Indigenista). The results have been mixed. About half of the families have been relocated in four resettlement zones at lower elevations (see Map 10), and appear to be slowly adjusting to a new way of life. But the remaining people have bitterly resented the "foreigners" and their interference, and have fled to the highlands to make their own way. For them the Papaloapan Project has meant not progress but untold misery.[6]

It was originally intended that the water impounded by the Alemán Dam would be used both for irrigation and power generation. However, the former objective was dropped during the Ruiz Cortines administration, while the job of building and operating the dam's power plant was assigned to the Federal Power Commission (Comisión Federal de Electricidad). Completed in 1960, this plant is

---

[6] For a detailed description of the early phases of the resettlement program and of some of the human problems that have arisen, see *11*, pp. 133–55 and *3*, pp. 205–26.

one of the largest in Latin America. Its four generators have a combined capacity of 154,000 kilowatts, over 10 per cent of the total
hydroelectric capacity installed in Mexico. Power is transmitted as
far as the city of Puebla in the Central Mesa. So far, however, the
demand is such that only one of the generators is regularly worked
on a full-time basis.

Looking to the future, the Commission hopes to construct a
number of additional flood-control dams. The largest of these is
projected for the Santo Domingo River, and for a site (Cerro de
Oro) that will enable its reservoir to be joined to that of the Alemán
Dam. The rationale behind this projected dam is that, although the
Papaloapan is reasonably well controlled for the moment, it is not
totally so, and conditions will change once the Alemán Dam's power
facility begins to generate at full capacity. The safe discharge capacity of the Papaloapan is now about 5,000 cubic meters per second
(up from about 3,500 in 1947), about the same as the maximum
expected flow of the Santo Domingo. Power generation and flood
control conflict in their requirements for reservoir management, and
after all four generators are in full operation, as much as 3,500 cubic
meters per second may have to be allowed through the Alemán Dam
during times of peak flow. To eliminate the possibility of serious
flooding at such times, the discharge of the Santo Domingo will have
to be reduced by at least as much.

Lesser dams are also planned for the Tesechoacan and San Juan
rivers, but they are accorded a relatively low priority because of the
limited areas they will protect. It will probably be many years before
they are constructed.

Agriculture

The most disappointing facet of the Papaloapan Project has been
the agricultural program. Unlike the flood-control and communications programs, this phase has suffered heavily as a result of the
Commission's many difficulties, and, although it has accounted for
12 per cent of the project's expenditures, it can point to few concrete
achievements.

The program has consisted of two general aspects, one of research and experimentation, the other of schemes designed to increase the area under cultivation. The latter (and more important) part of the program got off to an unfortunate beginning. We have noted that the Commission had originally intended to make its chief contribution to agricultural development in the form of supplemental irrigation and drainage. This emphasis is difficult to understand today, but in 1947 it was consistent with both the Alemán administration's policy of concentrating on overhead works and the inclinations of the Commission's key personnel. Like their colleagues in the Ministry of Hydraulic Resources, these officials were mostly civil engineers who had begun their careers in the irrigation zones of northern Mexico and who had become conditioned to thinking of land reclamation in terms of some form of water management. That they were now dealing with a tropical area in which the returns to irrigation would be comparatively minor seems to have been discounted, as was the fact that drainage would benefit only the most marginally productive lands. Nor do they seem to have been aware of the considerable technical problems that would be involved in conditioning the lateritic soils of the lowlands to support the type of year-round cropping needed to justify expensive irrigation works.

The principal agricultural scheme formulated during the first six years called for the development of an area of some 160,000 hectares, designated the Alemán Irrigation Zone, in the lowlands below the Alemán Dam (Map 10). The core of the project was to divert a portion of the water impounded by the dam to irrigate about two-thirds of the zone. A gravity-flow canal originating at the dam was to be the key structure.

But this scheme did not get much beyond the planning stage before it was rejected by the group that took over the Commission in December 1952. At that time it was turned down because of the great expense that would have been involved in building a gravity-flow canal through the foothills separating the dam from the area to be irrigated. Nevertheless, the idea that supplemental irrigation could be justified in a newly opened tropical region was not immediately abandoned, and two new lesser irrigation projects were started in 1953, one at Los Naranjos and one in the vicinity of the

Río Blanco.[7] The first was little more than a pilot project. Employing water pumped from the Tonto at a point well below the Alemán Dam, it was designed to irrigate a maximum of 4,000 hectares. The Río Blanco scheme was more ambitious. Built around two diversion dams, it was intended ultimately to irrigate 35,000 hectares.

These two schemes have accounted for about two-thirds of the Commission's investment in agriculture. By any standard, both have been failures. The venture at Los Naranjos proved uneconomic after two seasons (1955/56 and 1956/57) of small-scale operation, and was ended in 1957.[8] The Río Blanco scheme never really got started. After the diversion dams and main canals were built, it was discovered that the local cattlemen had no interest in seeing their holdings broken into small crop farms of questionable productivity. Most of them have refused to cooperate with the Commission, and only about 1,000 hectares in the zone have been brought under irrigation. The dams and canals stand today for the most part unused.

At about the same time that these ill-starred irrigation schemes were started, the Commission also embarked on a brief experience with credit and colonization. Several small colonization ventures had been begun during the final years of the Alemán administration. These were reorganized and expanded by the new officials, and, to finance their operations and those of other selected groups of smallholders, a program of agricultural lending soon took shape. Though modest in scope (in 1956, the last full year of operations, loans were made to only 1,200 farmers and the colonies included only about 550 families), these schemes began to loom larger in official thinking, until they became, in effect, pilot projects for the agricultural

[7] As the first step in developing the Alemán Irrigation Zone, the Commission was authorized in April 1950 to purchase or expropriate up to 28,000 hectares near the town of Los Naranjos. The 22,500 hectares obtained were designated the First Agricultural Development Unit, and the efforts to develop the Alemán Zone prior to 1953, mostly road building, were confined to it. With the abandonment of the original plan for the Alemán Irrigation Zone, its title was changed to refer only to the First Development Unit. To avoid confusing the two regions, I here refer to the smaller zone simply as Los Naranjos.

[8] The Commission's one drainage project, designed to reclaim some 3,000 hectares at Isla de Candelaria (near Tlacotalpan), also proved uneconomic, and was also abandoned in 1957.

phase of the 1955 revised development plan. They were, unfortunately, among the first casualties of the decision to cut back the Commission's activities. In 1957 both operations were drastically curtailed.

Although the research phase of the agricultural program began rather auspiciously, it too has failed to produce results commensurate with expenditures. In 1950 two experiment stations were established in the lowlands (one in the vicinity of Ciudad Alemán on alluvial soil, the other near Los Naranjos in an area typical of the plains between the rivers). Because there were then no other agricultural stations in tropical Mexico, the Commission initially received the full cooperation of the Ministry of Agriculture. This arrangement brought to the stations the skilled plant breeders of the Rockefeller Foundation, and several high-yielding strains of corn and rice were soon developed. Lamentably, this mutually advantageous arrangement lasted only until 1954, when the Ministry withdrew its support and established its own tropical station for the Foundation at Cotaxtla, just north of the basin. There followed a sharp deterioration in the caliber of the work done at the Commission's stations and a rapid turnover in their personnel. In 1957 the stations were transferred to the Ministry, only to be returned again two years later. Without the stability essential to sound experimentation, their recent contributions have been negligible.

Secondary Activities

The secondary activities in which the Commission has engaged to complement its main programs fall under the headings of sanitary engineering, education, and urban improvement. Because these efforts have involved modest outlays, they have benefited comparatively minor segments of the basin's population.

In the field of education, the Commission has concentrated on increasing the number of primary rural schools. Such schools, and teachers to man them, were in woefully short supply in 1947, when only about half of the children in the basin had the opportunity to attend classes. The Commission thus far has given financial aid for the construction or improvement of about 390 schools, with an enrollment of over 40,000 children. But much remains to be done; some 120,000 youngsters, or about 40 per cent of those of school age, live in areas that still have neither teachers nor schools (5, pp. 22, 57).

The Commission's sanitary-engineering operations have focused on reducing the incidence of the two principal maladies afflicting the basin's population, malaria and the various intestinal parasites caused by polluted drinking water. In 1947 malaria was endemic through-out most of the tierra caliente, while virtually the entire rural population suffered from one or more types of internal parasites. Since then, over 160,000 people have benefited from the construction of some 70 sanitary water systems, and the incidence of malaria has been sharply reduced. Through 1956 the Commission maintained a number of teams to spray dwellings with a residual type of DDT. Although this activity was taken away from the Commission in the following year, it has been continued as part of the Ministry of Health's nation-wide anti-malaria drive.

About the expenditures for urban improvement little can be said. Most of the outlays under this heading have gone into building Ciudad Alemán, the Commission's headquarters town. But a few parks, streets, and recreational facilities have been constructed in other communities. They are best justified on political grounds.

A BRIEF ASSESSMENT

Unfortunately, it is not possible to quantify in any detail the over-all benefits that have accrued as a result of these various activities. Not until the findings of the 1960 Censuses become available will one be able to get a reasonably full picture of the human and economic changes that have taken place in the basin, and for these we shall have to wait several more years.[9] Still, there is no doubt that the changes have been impressive. This much is apparent to the eye. The lower basin, especially, presents a vastly different aspect than it did just a decade and a half ago. Its towns are obviously

---

[9] The full findings of the 1950 Census of Agriculture for the states in which the basin falls were not published until 1958.

prospering and growing in size, while along its new system of roads one notes increasing numbers of buses and trucks. Without a doubt the region is now a part of the thriving national economy. And if the upper basin's hinterland still lags well behind, it is at least beginning to stir from its centuries of isolation.

Agriculture, of course, has been the principal beneficiary. Thanks to the new roads and the reduction in flooding, the area under exploitation in the lowlands has gone up sharply. The area planted to sugar cane (one of the few crops for which reasonably reliable annual data are available) more than doubled during the project's first decade (6, pp. 248–58), while less trustworthy estimates suggest that the area under all crops has expanded at an annual rate of about 7 per cent.[10] Other sectors have also responded. Tuxtepec is now the home of a modern newsprint mill (the first major industrial facility to be built to take advantage of the new supply of power), and the timber stands of the upper basin are beginning to be exploited on a commercial basis.

These elements add up to a noteworthy start toward sustained growth. One cannot but feel, nonetheless, that it is less of a start than would have been made if the agricultural phase of the Commission's program had been more rationally conceived and executed.

CITATIONS

1 Roxana Arce Ybarra, "La navegación fluvial en el sistema del río Papaloapan" (Comisión del Papaloapan, March 1955, unpublished).

2 "Bosquejo de un programa total, 1955–1970" (Comisión del Papaloapan, September 1955, unpublished).

3 Fernando Camara, "Déplacement et réistallation de groupes indigénes au Mexique," *Civilisations*, V, No. 2, 1955.

4 Combined Mexican Working Party, *The Economic Development of*

---

[10] These estimates (cf. *6*, pp. 185–94; *7*, facing p. 88), prepared by the Commission's personnel, used as their starting point the notoriously unreliable figures of the Directorate of Rural Economics of the Ministry of Agriculture. As anyone who has worked with Mexican agricultural statistics knows, the annual estimates of the Directorate cannot be reconciled with the more trustworthy findings of the decennial censuses, and most serious workers try to limit their use of them. In the present instance they probably overstate the rate at which crop production in the lower basin has increased.

Mexico (International Bank for Reconstruction and Development, Baltimore, 1953).

5 Mexico, Sec. Rec. Hid., Comisión del Papaloapan, *Breves apuntes acerca de la cuenca del Papaloapan y de la labor realizada por la Comisión* (1959).

6 Mexico, Sec. Rec. Hid., Comisión del Papaloapan, *Compendio estadístico de la cuenca, 1960.*

7 Mexico, Sec. Rec. Hid., Comisión del Papaloapan, *Economía del Papaloapan: Evaluación de las inversiones y sus efectos* (1958).

8 J. S. Noriega, "Control del río Papaloapan: Preparación del plan de estudios definitivos y programa de construcción de las obras," *Ingeniería hidráulica en México,* I, April–June 1947 (part 1) ; and *ibid.,* I, July–September 1947 (part 2).

9 Fernando Rosenzweig Hernandez, "El programa de crédito agrícola de la Comisión del Papaloapan" (Comisión del Papaloapan, March 1957, unpublished).

10 Alfonso Villa Rojas, *El Papaloapan: Obra del presidente Alemán, 1947–1952* (Comisión del Papaloapan, 1952).

11 Alfonso Villa Rojas, *Los Mazatecos y el problema indigena de la cuenca del Papaloapan* (Memorias del Instituto Nacional Indigenista, vol. VII, México, D. F., 1955).

Chapter 7

THE PILOT AGRICULTURAL SCHEMES

Although the Commission can look back on few positive accomplishments in the field of agricultural development, it would be a mistake to write off this aspect of the Papaloapan Project as a total loss. For, though the cost was high, a number of valuable lessons were learned while the credit and colonization schemes were in operation. Properly appreciated, this backlog of experience can point the way toward a sounder course of action in the future, both in the basin and in Mexico's other tropical areas.

The Commission's experience with credit and colonization was relatively brief. Not until 1953 did either program get under way in earnest, and both were among the first activities to be affected by the decision to cut back the Commission's peripheral projects. By 1957 they had ceased to be viable experiments, and the subsequent attention given them was mainly of a salvaging nature. The following tabulation of the Commission's credit outlays is indicative of this course of events (7, Table 2):

Year	Loans (*Thousand pesos*)
1951	63
1952	1
1953	857
1954	943
1955	3,303
1956	5,905
1957	3,054
1958	556
1959	26

The credit and colonization operations were, in effect, pilot projects. In comparison with the Commission's main development works, neither involved many people nor a great investment, and it came

123

to be accepted as the 1955 revised development plan took shape in official thinking that the specific mechanics of its agricultural phase would be drawn from their experience. The schemes were not, however, pilot projects in the sense of being controlled experiments executed consistently from the outset. Rather, like so many aspects of the Papaloapan Project, they were begun in response to certain needs of the moment and evolved from there. The credit operation thus grew out of the need to finance the colonization program, and later was broadened to include selected groups of established smallholders. The colonization program, on the other hand, included aspects of the Alemán reservoir resettlement operation as well as colonization proper.

Because of this lack of internal consistency, the lessons of the programs can best be brought out not by a comprehensive chronology—which would unduly emphasize organizational deficiencies and changes—but by the experience of key individual projects. In this connection, three schemes stand apart from the rest. Two of them (Los Naranjos and Michapan) were concerned with colonizaation, the other (Valle Nacional) with granting credit to established smallholders to enable them to expand their operations. Not only were these schemes among the first to be initiated; in 1956, the last full year of operations, they together accounted for about two-thirds of the individuals receiving credit from the Commission and for over 70 per cent of the colonists settled under its auspices.

COLONIZATION

Los Naranjos and Michapan

Despite a great difference in size—Los Naranjos included 22,500 hectares, Michapan only a little more than 1,400—and the fact that they were situated some 80 miles apart (Map 10), the schemes at Los Naranjos and Michapan had much in common. Both were located in the plains between the rivers of the lower basin, the principal component of the unexploited portions of the basin's tierra caliente; both involved tracts that were opened up as a result of the Commission's activities and were previously all but devoid of population and cultivated land; and both were originally conceived as combination supplemental-irrigation and colonizaton projects during the Alemán administration.

With reference to the last point, the tract at Los Naranjos was originally intended to be the pilot unit of the Alemán Irrigation Zone. After this project was dropped by the Ruiz Cortines administration, the area was selected as the site for the smaller of the two supplemental-irrigation facilities actually built. Despite this apparent emphasis on reclamation through irrigation, however, Los Naranjos accumulated little experience in this regard. Its irrigation system was operated for only two seasons (the winters of 1955/56 and 1956/57) before being abandoned as uneconomic, and only about 350 hectares were ever artificially watered. Instead, the experience dealt almost entirely with the settlement and development of land under conditions of seasonal agriculture.

The direct involvement of the Commission at Los Naranjos began in April 1950, when it was authorized by Presidential decree to purchase or expropriate up to 28,000 hectares in the area. The 22,500 hectares set aside under this authorization were then virtually unexploited. To judge from detailed surveys of some 6,400 hectares in the tract's northwestern portion, the population supported was of the order of only 3.5 persons per square mile, and the cultivated area a mere 2 per cent of the total. As in the interfluvial plains generally, the great bulk of the land was either devoted to extensive livestock pasturage or not used at all (*6*, p. 3; *5*, p. 32).

Efforts to develop the area proceeded rather slowly at first. Because of the time required to negotiate the transfer of property titles and to construct the necessary access roads, settlement was not begun until the closing months of 1952. One colony was started at that time, and thereafter the tempo of activity picked up. By 1956 five colonies, with a combined area of almost 3,300 hectares (roughly half of it under cultivation) and almost 225 participating families, had been formed.[1] Names and areas, together with the year in which

---

[1] Strictly speaking, a total of seven colonies were then in existence at Los Naranjos. But two of them (Plan de Oro and Ruiz Cortines) operated only briefly as true colonies, and therefore are not considered here.

they were established in the zone, and the number of families as of
April 1956, appear in the following summarization (2; 7, pp. 20–33):

Colony	Year established	Hectares assigned	Families
Zapata	1952	557	18
Oaxaca	1953	339	27
Los Naranjos	1954	511	56
Resumidero	1954	784	73
Independencia	1954	1,096	48
Total		3,287	222

All of the colonies were situated in the southwestern corner of the
zone, chiefly in the area circumscribed by the main access road.
Except for Independencia, which included the area with irrigation,
all were dependent on natural rainfall.

In contrast to Los Naranjos, where settlement had been extended
to only a fraction of the available area by 1956, virtually all of the
smaller tract at Michapan was so allocated. With 80 families in April
of that year, Michapan's one colony was cultivating almost 900 of
the 1,422 hectares assigned to it.

The scheme at Michapan, somewhat incongruously, had its origin in the public-health program. As one of its first sanitary-engineering works, the Commission undertook to provide the town of
Acayucan with modern water and sewage systems. Because ground-
water conditions in the immediate vicinity of Acayucan were un-
satisfactory, these systems were to utilize water diverted from a creek
about 10 miles away. Included in the project, accordingly, was the
construction of a small diversion dam and transmission canal.

Both the dam and the canal were situated in largely unexploited
country. Some time after their construction had been begun, it was
decided to expand the project to include colonizing and irrigating a
portion of the land opened up by the access road paralleling the
canal.[2] As the pilot unit for this venture, the tract at Michapan was
acquired in 1950. But work on this aspect of the scheme was slow
to begin, and by mid-1952, when the water and sewage systems were
in operation, about all that could be reported was that the tract had

[2] This road is now part of the Gulf highway.

been surveyed and the locations for the distributory canals determined.

As at Los Naranjos, the winter of 1952/53 saw a sharp change at Michapan. Instead of continuing to delay colonization pending construction of the irrigation facilities, the Commission's new officials determined to begin settlement immediately. The zone was ordered resurveyed, and within months the first group of colonists was brought in. Both 1954 and 1955 witnessed the arrival of additional settlers, with the result that by 1956, as noted, the greater part of the zone was given over to colonization. As to irrigation works, nothing was done; this phase of the scheme was dropped without really having been begun.

The Approach

Although organized colonization ventures can and have taken a great variety of forms, most of the governmental-sponsored schemes recently initiated in the humid tropics may be thought of as having been carried out under one or the other of two opposing schools of thought. One of these, which might be termed the "self-help" school, holds that colonists cannot be helped permanently if more is done for them than they could ultimately do for themselves, and that therefore the government should extend only a minimum of aid. It should, of course, assist with such essential overhead services as roads, schools, sanitary water supplies, and secure titles to the land, but otherwise its role should be passive. The settler should clear his land himself, build his own house, and generally provide for his own needs as his resources accumulate. Rapid results and immediate marketable surpluses, it is admitted, would be neither expected nor forthcoming, but progress would be sure; and the settler would have the satisfaction of personal achievement in making a new life for himself.

A very different view is advanced by those adhering to the other, or "paternalistic," school. They hold that although any progress achieved through self-help would indeed be secure, there would probably never be much of it, because of the difficulties of resource accumulation under the traditional systems of tropical agriculture. Stressing the theoretical advantage of comparatively heavy initial capitalization—and, insofar as tropical farming systems are concerned, of revolution over evolution—they contend that both quicker and more positive results would be forthcoming if the government were to anticipate virtually all of the colonist's operational requirements and undertake to supply him with something approaching a complete "farm in being" and enough follow-up aid and guidance to enable him to operate it efficiently. Under this school, the land is typically cleared by the government with either machinery or hired labor, and the settler is endowed with enough equipment (formerly animal-powered, but now frequently motorized) to permit immediate exploitation. The costs of such schemes are naturally quite high, and even their most outspoken proponents admit that the settler is confronted with a heavy initial burden of debt. But this drawback, it is argued, is more than offset by his being able to begin at once to farm on a commercial scale and at near his optimum capability for debt retirement.

The general approach followed by the Commission at Michapan and at most of the colonies at Los Naranjos was that of the paternalistic school.[3] In addition to providing such overhead facilities as roads, schools, and drinking water, an attempt was made to introduce efficient, commercial-scale agriculture. The colonizing families were sold cleared (or soon-to-be-cleared) plots of land on long-term credit, and were installed in ready-built houses. Shorter-term loans were provided to cover the day-to-day expenses of crop production. Power equipment was made available for the more labor-consuming operations. And close supervision and technical guidance were supplied.

This is not to suggest that identical procedures were followed with all of the colonies. Because of the inevitable individual circumstances, there were differences both between Michapan and Los

[3] Legal requirements to the contrary, the paternalistic approach was not forced upon the Commission. The 1946 Colonization Law, which was in force when the Commission's colonies were formed, required that a colonizing agency clear the land, divide it into individual plots, build access facilities, and generally "ensure that the colonies are established with all the economic resources necessary to bring about effective agricultural operations." But in practice these requirements were usually ignored; the National Colonization Commission and its successor, the Department of Agrarian Affairs and Colonization, have typically limited themselves to giving little more than legal birth to their colonies.

Naranjos and among the several colonies at Los Naranjos. In most instances, however, these differences were ones of detail (e.g., the amount of land given each settler, the cropping pattern followed, or the manner in which machinery was made available); except for Resumidero colony, which because of a unique set of circumstances was left largely to its own devices, the essential format of paternalism was the same.[4]

The procedure that came to be followed called for a thorough program of preparation. When a tract was designated for settlement, the Commission undertook to ready it fully for immediate exploitation. Its crews surveyed the area, built the necessary roads, and dug at least one well. Then the land was cleared and stumped with power machinery, and blocked off into individual units. By the time the settlers arrived, the unit was entirely laid out and readied for cultivation, in some later cases even to the point of being plowed.

Following the settlement pattern of the traditional Mexican village, the colonies were laid out in two sections. The smaller of these, generally located near the center of the colony and along its main road, made up the "urban" portion. Each urban area had its heart in a small community center, made up of a school, a town hall, and a well, built and supplied free by the Commission. The adjacent residential section was divided into lots averaging about .5 hectare in

---

[4] Resumidero colony was started in the spring of 1952 under the auspices of the National Colonization Commission. It is described as having been formed by a group of "veterans of the Revolution," but almost half of its membership was soon made up of a company of Protestant converts who, with the assistance of an American missionary, were seeking a new life away from their former homes in the highlands of Oaxaca. The colony was first established along the road leading to the Alemán Dam, in the general area where most of the people displaced by the dam's reservoir were being resettled. The site had not yet been officially surveyed, a prerequisite to permanent possession, but it was thought that this would be taken care of within a month or two. Not until two and a half years later, however, did the surveyors actually arrive. In the meantime, the Commission had decided that it needed the tract for the resettlement effort, and refused to let the colonists to stay on. But by way of compensation, it offered to move the colony, by then reduced to 73 members, to a new site in the Los Naranjos zone, and to give it free land there.

Because of these unusual circumstances, the procedure followed with Resumidero differed sharply from the norm. As with the other colonies, the Commission blocked off the new site into individual units and provided a school, a community building, and a well, but otherwise left the colonists on their own. They cleared the land themselves, built their own houses, and received neither loans nor technical guidance.

size (large enough for a family garden, a flock of chickens, and perhaps a hog or two), each of which was equipped with a simple but attractive house constructed of milled lumber and palm thatching.

The plots into which the surrounding farm land was delimited were also of modest size, averaging in most cases slightly over 10 hectares. This size was selected arbitrarily (there was then hardly any evidence on which to base a more sophisticated procedure), and about all that can be said about it is that it reflected the Commission's intention that the colonies be operated exclusively as crop farms and that they might eventually receive irrigation. It was assumed that with partial mechanization and other modern techniques the plots would prove adequate for commercial-scale production. Their apportionment (together with that of an associated urban lot), one to a family, was determined by a drawing upon the colonists' arrival.

In contrast to the relatively thorough preparations made in anticipation of their arrival, the colonists themselves were given little advance attention. Prior screening was minimal, with provision instead being made for the early elimination of undesirables. Instead of granting immediate ownership to the newcomer, the Commission signed a "settlement agreement" with him. This agreement granted him rent-free tenure for a period of a year, in exchange for his agreeing to follow any instructions with respect to his agricultural operations. If, at the end of this probationary period, he had evidenced the willingness and capability to farm his plot satisfactorily, he was offered a purchase contract; if not, he was expelled from the colony.[5]

The purchase contracts were essentially long-term loans. The colonist was expected to pay only 10 per cent of the total cost of his plot at the time he signed the contract. The balance was payable in as many as ten yearly installments. Despite the high risk, the rate of interest was moderate: 6 per cent on the balance outstanding, except in cases of default, when it was increased to 9. The contracts were guaranteed by a mortgage in the Commission's favor, and in

---

[5] Before he was offered a purchase contract, the settler was supposed to pass an inspection, the key criterion of which was that 80 per cent of his plot be under cultivation. But in practice the outcome hinged largely on whether he cooperated with the Commission's field men and was liked by them.

addition by a continuance of its voice in land management. Though given title, the buyers agreed neither to "dispose, mortgage, transfer, nor encumber" their plots without the Commission's approval, and to continue obeying any instructions with respect to cropping and soil conservation practices.

Because the Commission expected to recover most of its initial direct investment in the colonies, the prices specified in the contracts were high. Although charges varied on a per hectare basis from as little as 400 pesos to as much as 1,600, the average price for a fully prepared unit was about 1,100 pesos per hectare ($88), about ten times the cost of the unimproved land to the Commission. The greater part of this difference could be ascribed to clearing and stumping; the cost of the roads, houses, and other direct improvements averaged out to only about 300 pesos per hectare.

High though these prices were for the area, the Commission's planners nevertheless thought them justified by the land's immediate earning capacity. Just what this capacity was no one could say with certainty. Improbable as it may seem, especially in view of the number of years that intervened between the Commission's initial involvement in the zones and the arrival of the first colonists, no preliminary experiments were conducted at either Los Naranjos or Michapan. It was confidently assumed, however, that with either of the two main crops programmed—corn at Michapan, rice at Los Naranjos— the colonists would have no difficulty meeting their production, amortization, and living expenses: provided, of course, that they were able to utilize their entire units effectively.

The second, or follow-up, phase of the Commission's approach, through which this proviso was to be met, had its basis in parallel and closely coordinated programs of credit and partial mechanization. The new settlers, who generally arrived a few months before the start of the cropping cycle in the spring, were advanced credits (amounting on the average to about 700 pesos per hectare) to meet the costs of their first crop and to cover their living expenses until harvest time.[6] If they stayed on after their probationary year, these short-term, or *avío*, loans were renewed each spring and were some-

[6] The early colonists at Michapan, whose lands were not initially cleared, also received advances during their first year to enable clearing to be done.

times supplemented by longer-term *refaccionario* advances for the purchase of work stock, farm implements, and the like.[7] It was intended that these credits would be granted until the colonist had either established himself to the extent that he could obtain commercial financing at a reasonable cost or accumulated enough capital to underwrite his operations himself.

The loans were extended on a "supervised" basis; that is, they were not unrestricted advances to be used entirely as the colonists saw fit, but were accompanied by both supervision and technical guidance and, as a corollary, control. Supervised credit, or—as applied by the Commission perhaps more descriptively—"training" credit, differs from normal credit in several respects, the most important of which is its essentially social objective. It is generally granted only to persons whose resources or immediate prospects, or both, are so limited that they cannot obtain funds elsewhere. By combining technical aid and training with credit, its key feature, it aims to raise the output and income levels of such persons so that they may ultimately qualify for more conventional financing. The Commission's loan program was thus intended more as a means than an end, and had many aspects of direct subsidization. The interest charges, 6 per cent for refaccionario loans and 9 per cent for avío, were quite moderate by local standards, and were intended to cover only those costs that could not properly be ascribed to extension work.

Although the concept of supervised credit was by no means new with the Commission, its application in Latin America previously had been very limited. The officials of the Commission considered that theirs were among the first true experiments with it in Mexico.

No less an innovation and equally untried was the other aspect of the follow-up approach, that of making power machinery available for the more labor-consuming operations. This program was motivated by the desire that the colonies operate on a commercial basis

---

[7] The avío loan, granted for periods of up to 18 months and secured by a crop lien, differs from the production loan of the United States in that it is commonly intended to cover the living expenses of the borrower as well as his direct yearly outlays for crop production. The longer-term refaccionario loan is the counterpart of the American intermediate-term capital improvement loan.

from the outset. With the traditional systems of farming of the tierra caliente, including the ox-drawn wooden plow variation as well as the basic system of fire agriculture, this was considered out of the question. Even with the land fully cleared, local experience suggested that the maximum crop area an individual could exploit yearly should be reckoned at between two and four hectares, little more than that needed to produce his family's requirements; and given the apparent inability of either of the traditional systems to fully control the spread of weeds, it was reasoned that without machinery, much of the land would soon revert to bush cover.

As far as day-to-day operations were concerned, the mechanization program was considered a part of the assistance provided through the credit program, and was administered as such at both Los Naranjos and Michapan. The more formal methods followed, however, differed between the two zones. At Michapan the equipment was purchased cooperatively by the settlers with refaccionario credit supplied by the Commission; in the Los Naranjos zone it was made available on a custom basis. A central machinery station was established at a point convenient to the colonies, and plowing and other mechanical services were supplied the settlers, who paid for them with funds received as avío loans.

But these inter-scheme differences were of little practical significance. In both zones the essentials were the same: the equipment was financed through the credit program, and its use was controlled through the comprehensive technical guidance afforded with the loans. Agricultural residencies were established at both zones, and full-time field supervisors were assigned to work closely with the colonists. Because commercially oriented, semi-mechanized production was totally new to the bulk of the settlers, the responsibilities of these field men cannot be overemphasized. In effect, they were called upon to assume almost complete charge of the colonists' operations.

This situation was of course wholly consistent with the general policy of paternalism being followed by the Commission. Though in theory the colonies were made up of independent freeholders, the Commission operated on the assumption that until the settlers had become well established and fully adjusted to their new environment, their interests could best be served by concentrating the decision-making power in the hands of the Commission. As both types of land-alienation contract expressly reserved for the Commission a substantial voice—which amounted to veto power—over land use, so did the loan agreement, the chief instrument governing the follow-up activities. Almost without exception, these agreements had annexed "calendars of operations" setting forth in detail what crops would be grown, when planting would take place, and what implements and cultural practices would be employed. The granting of credit was made contingent upon satisfactory compliance with these calendars; hence the Commission was in a position to exercise complete control over the agriculture of the colonies, and to impose at will whatever decisions it considered to be to the colonists' advantage.

The Experience in Brief

Mid-1957 marked the end of Los Naranjos and Michapan as viable colonization experiments. In line with the decision to cut back the Commission's peripheral activities, the credit program was drastically curtailed, and—in an attempt to enable the Commission to withdraw with some grace from the field of colonization—the settlers were offered title to their holdings if they would pay off their accumulated indebtedness plus 25 per cent of the value of the land. Because few were in a position to do so, the net effect of this "regularization" was to cause the great majority of the colonists[8] to abandon their plots and seek their fortunes elsewhere. The attention given the colonies since then has centered around efforts to salvage something from the debris.

But even before these events took place, both Los Naranjos and Michapan were in serious trouble. Between the winter of 1952/53 and January 1956, the Commission settled a total of 424 families in the two zones (ex-Resumidero colony). In April 1956 a census revealed that of this number, 195, or 46 per cent, had either given up and left or been dropped by the authorities (*2; 12*, p. 38). Unfortunately, there are no available data from which to make a breakdown

---

[8] Excepting those at Resumidero colony, who had received their holdings free.

of how many had abandoned their plots and how many were expelled during their probationary year. I am reliably informed, however, that the majority, perhaps as many as 80 or 90 per cent, left of their own accord.

The experience of the credit program was equally inauspicious. Of some 4.1 million pesos advanced in the form of avío loans between the summers of 1953 and 1956, no less than 35 per cent had been written off by the end of 1956 as unrecoverable. And this was not all. Of the nearly 250 colonists who had received loans in 1956, it was expected that about 100 would have to be dropped during the following year as "having been catalogued definitely as poor credit risks" and the program continued with only 143 families (93 at Los Naranjos, 50 at Michapan) (*12*, p. 38, Table 9).

Even before the schemes collapsed, then, the mere *hope* of success was held for only a third of the participants—in view of the nature of the Commission's program, a poor showing indeed. Only at Resumidero, the one colony that had been left to sink or swim on its own, could the experience be considered promising. Of its 73 members, just two had dropped out, and these were immediately replaced by newcomers.

An Evaluation

What went wrong? Outwardly, at least, the Commission would seem to have laid a solid foundation for successful settlement. Land, shelter, equipment, working capital, guidance—generous provision was made for each. A visitor to either Los Naranjos or Michapan betweeen 1953 and 1956 could not have helped being impressed by the physical contrasts between the colonies and the surrounding countryside. In the one were schools, neat rows of dwellings, cleared fields, and modern farm implements; in the other, an impoverished peasantry continued to farm scattered clearings with little more than the machete and the hoe. How, then, did it happen that the schemes did not meet with more success?

It goes without saying that the explanation is not simple. Colonization schemes, involving as they do both human and technical inputs, are subject to a wide range of interacting influences, any one or a combination of which might conceivably determine failure instead of success. If these influences are to be fully unraveled and those of critical importance earmarked and assigned precise values, a vast amount of evidence is called for. Such evidence is rarely available to the degree that one would wish, and the present instance is no exception. (The Commission's records leave much to be desired.) Still, it seems clear that the basic weaknesses of the schemes were (1) the colonists themselves and the method of their selection, and (2) the manner in which the follow-up phase of the paternalistic approach was carried out.

Regarding the first shortcoming (which was the less important of the two), we have noted that relatively little advanced attention was given to the question of the colonists themselves. For the most part they were chosen not because of any noteworthy qualifications they might possess, but simply because they had petitioned the government for assistance. Though colonization under the Commission's auspices did not begin until late 1952, much publicity was given during the early years of the Papaloapan Project to the expected achievements in this field. In March 1947, for instance, a leading national weekly quoted the Minister of Hydraulic Resources to the effect that "hundreds of thousands of people will be able to settle and live prosperously in a region that will be the richest in Mexico" (*13*, p. 14). Groups of land-short peasants from all over the country responded to this and similar pronouncements in the traditional manner of Mexico, with an appeal to the President or some other high official. Therefore, when colonization was actually started, the Commission was confronted with a bulky sheaf of applications, many of which were accompanied by notes from the President's Office requesting that something be done to assist the petitioners.

The decision to draw settlers chiefly from among these applicants (and to rely on the probationary technique for the weeding out of undesirables) had several consequences. In the first place, it caused the colonies initially to be populated almost entirely with persons whose contact with the tierra caliente had been minimal. The publicity about the Commission was directed to the entire country. However, because of the heavy concentration of the population in the uplands and the rural overcrowding there (and perhaps also because of a natural inclination for temperate-zone dwellers to be more susceptible to visions of a tropical paradise), it appealed primarily to highlanders, and these made up the bulk of those first receiving consideration. Of the original company of 43 families settled at Michapan, 25 came from the Laguna area of the Northern Mesa, an irrigated cotton-growing region about as unlike the lower basin in both climate and agriculture as can be found in Mexico. At Los Naranjos the first colonies were established mainly with families from in and around the Central Mesa, notably from the states of Tlaxcala, Morelos, and Guerrero.

Some of the Commission's officials have claimed that this initial preponderance of highlanders was the prime cause of failure, arguing that most of the colonists who left did so because they were unable to adapt themselves to the heat and humidity of the coastal plain. However, the evidence does not support this contention. One of the later colonies at Los Naranjos was settled with families from the immediate vicinity, and it enjoyed no greater success than the others; and Resumidero, the one promising colony, was composed largely of highlanders. Still, there can be no doubt that the highlanders' ignorance of tropical farming methods introduced yet another unknown into an already complicated equation, and made the heavy tasks confronting the Commission's field supervisors even more difficult.

Nor can there be any doubt about the other unfavorable consequences of the Commission's selection process. Many of the colonists accepted were psychologically unprepared for the trials that lay ahead. They were shocked by the realities of pioneer life (even as ameliorated by the Commission) and quickly became discouraged. In addition, some of those accepted were nothing but adventurers who had seen in the Commission's promise of financial aid an easy means of getting something for nothing. When this did not prove the case, they promptly withdrew, but not without first having exercised a disruptive influence.

A final consequence of the mode of selection was the extraordinary variety in the membership of the colonies. Although at the outset each colony was formed with a fairly homogeneous company of settlers (most of the petitions had been received from groups rather than individuals), the composition of the colonies became increasingly mixed as replacements were brought in for those who left. To the remnants of the party from the Laguna area at Michapan, for instance, were added 25 families from around Teotitlán in the upper basin, as well as several different groups from the eastern part of the coastal plain. Here, as at Los Naranjos, mistrust among the settlers and other forms of intra-colony strife were the result.

Nevertheless, the consequences of poor selection should not be overrated. Whatever their deficiencies as a group, most of the colonists accepted were ready and willing to work hard at making new lives for themselves. For these persons any explanation of failure must take into account the program of paternalism into which they were expected to fit. This program, particularly in its follow-up phase, proved anything but effective. In fact, instead of hastening the development of the colonists into self-reliant commercial growers, certain aspects of the approach clearly impeded it.

Criticism may be leveled against the follow-up operations at Los Naranjos and Michapan under two general headings: the manner in which guidance was afforded the colonists, and the content of this guidance. As to the first of these, the Commission's policy in regard to technical assistance has been outlined. Because semi-mechanized, commercially oriented production would be new to the colonists, and because many of them were unfamiliar with the tropical environment of the coastal plain, it was assumed that in the beginning their interests would be best furthered if the Commission were to exercise a powerful voice over the operation of their holdings. In theory, the concept embodied here was commendable: the colonist, guided during his first years, would quickly learn through experience how to manage his plot. But in practice nothing of the sort obtained. Rather than readying the settler for individual entrepreneurship, the direction was administered in a way that could only stifle his enterprise and foster a feeling of dependency on outside help.

In the first place, the colonists were allowed only the smallest latitude for exercising individual judgment and initiative. It has been noted that compulsory "calendars of operations" were appended to the loan agreements. Instead of being relatively general and permitting the colonist a degree of personal leeway, these calendars were comprehensive in the extreme—to the point not only of specifying what crops would be grown and under what system of cultivation, but of spelling out in detail how the various operations were to be performed.

Moreover, the calendars were imposed without regard to the differences among the settlers. The field supervisors made few attempts to consult them in advance, or to fashion individual programs consistent with their special desires and abilities. Plans typically were drawn up on a colony-wide or even scheme-wide basis, and as a result the energetic and promising colonists were treated the same as the dull and the lazy. In the case of the 1956 summer crop at Los Naranjos, for instance, every settler in every colony was required to plant 90 per cent of his land to rice and the remainder to corn (*4*, p. 1). For all the influence his skill and aspirations could have over the management of his plot, the enterprising colonist might almost have been a laborer working on a plantation operated by the Commission.

But this total domination of the colonist, it should be hastily added, can only be regarded as a secondary failing of the follow-up approach. Far more crucial—and here we come to what was undoubtedly the principal cause of the scheme's failure—was the content of the guidance. Indeed, most of the settlers would probably have dismissed the administrative procedures as temporary irritants if it had been apparent to them that the orders were sound and working to their advantage. Unfortunately, hardly any such evidence was to be had. After having been but a few months in either zone, the colonist could not have failed to suspect that something was basically wrong with the Commission's direction.

And there was. In neither zone was colonization preceded by a period of preliminary experimenting. True, one of the Commission's two agricultural stations had been set up in 1950 a few miles from Los Naranjos, but its personnel had been mainly engaged in plant breeding. No attempt was made to simulate expected operating conditions. The first colonists arrived before anything had been learned about likely yields, methods of maintaining soil fertility, the local suitability of various types of machinery, and similar matters critical to the planning of a sound system of farm management. Because there were no established nuclei of sedentary cultivation elsewhere in the interfluvial plains, the Commission was unable to compensate for this deficiency by drawing on the experience of nearby regions. Coupled with the avowed goal of introducing not traditional but semi-mechanized agriculture into the colonies, this circumstance had far-reaching repercussions. Instead of being in a position to order combinations of crops and cultural systems whose practicability under local conditions had already been proved, the Commission was forced to operate the colonies essentially as experimental farms and to formulate its instructions around the presumptions of its agricultural and colonizational staffs. Inevitably, mistakes and unforeseen complications were numerous.

Basic to many of the difficulties was the mechanization program. Again for purposes of illustration, consider the 1956 Los Naranjos summer crop. As in previous years the principal crop was rice, the colonists having been informed that nine of every ten hectares were to be so planted. A total of 1,504 hectares was earmarked for production. The land was to be prepared, and in some instances planted, with the equipment of the machinery station. The month of May was set aside for this work; but, as it turned out, at least two months would have been needed. Many of the tractors (most of which proved too light for the work to be done) broke down and had to spend precious days in the shop. When the rains began, only about 500 hectares had been readied. Though yields on this land were quite encouraging (1.5 tons per hectare), heavy losses were unavoidable. Of an avío advance of 382,000 pesos, only 269,000 pesos were repaid.

A similar situation obtained on a smaller scale at Independencia colony during the preceding winter season. Here for the first time some 300 hectares had been linked to the pilot irrigation system. Great hopes were held for this system, and the entire tract was programmed for immediate cropping, half of it to corn, and 65 and 85 hectares to rice and beans, respectively. A total of 320,000 pesos in avío credit was advanced to finance operations. It was planned that planting would take place in November, when in future seasons it might be expected that the summer crop would be harvested. Because of an almost inconceivable combination of misunderstandings, delays, and breakdowns, however, the machinery station did not actually complete planting until the end of January. Given the growing period of the crops involved (about six months for rice, four for corn, and three for beans), the outcome was inevitable. When the rainy season set in some four months later, only the beans had had time to mature and be harvested. Both corn and rice had to be written off as a total loss, "to the cause of experience"—as the official idiom had by then come to have it—as did some 206,000 pesos of the avío advance.

But not all of the problems arose from the mechanization effort. Important losses were occasioned by errors in crop selection and by just plain poor judgment. The 1955 season at Michapan provides an example of both. As the Los Naranjos colonies were generally planted to rice, so the greater part of the land at Michapan was given over to corn. While these crops (after a year or two) offered the advantage of familiarity, some of the field men were rightly distressed that the colonists were obliged to risk all on the success of just one. Thus it was when a new supervisor arrived at Michapan in 1955. Determined to diversify, he ordered planted (without any prior testing) no less than 174 hectares of peanuts in addition to corn. The decision proved disastrous. The crop responded poorly to the soils of the area; even the supervisor lacked prior experience in its cultivation. The result: almost complete failure, with but 27,000 pesos of an avío credit of 201,000 pesos recovered (12, p. 39, Appendix Table C).

Perhaps tolerable singly, in combination these complications and mistakes had a decisive influence where it mattered most—on the colonists' income. Not a year went by at any colony without at least one unexpected complication arising, and whereas it had been anticipated that the colonists' returns would easily exceed their production and land amortization outlays (by up to 1,000 pesos per hectare according to one forecast), just the opposite occurred. Though there are no available figures from which a series of income estimates can be derived, it is indicative that not once during the entire 1953–56 interval were the Michapan colonists as a whole able to repay their avío loans, while at Los Naranjos only those of one colony (Independencia) managed to do so and this during just one season (the summer of 1955) (*12*, Table 9).

With many if not most of their number consistently unable to earn enough to cover their production and living expenses, let alone their long-term obligations, and hence consistently forced to seek at least a partial remission of their annual debt in order to subsist until the following season, a convincing explanation for the high turnover in colonists presents itself. Viewed against such a backdrop, what seems surprising is not that so many colonists became discouraged and left, but that so many stayed on as long as they did. The Mexican peasant will tolerate much for an opportunity to improve himself.

CREDIT

In contrast to Los Naranjos and Michapan, the third of the Commission's main pilot agricultural projects, Valle Nacional, was comparatively uncomplicated. Concerned with the problems involved in directly assisting established smallholders to expand their commercial operations, it involved only the extension of credit. It lends itself therefore to relatively brief description.

Valle Nacional

Unlike most other parts of the Papaloapan basin, which either have no commercial tradition or have begun only recently to produce for the market, the area around the town of Valle Nacional enjoys a rather long history of commercial cropping. Tobacco was grown there commercially even before the rail network was completed, and achieved great importance around the turn of the century. Though production has since fallen off sharply, tobacco is still the area's chief source of cash income, and it was with the tobacco growers that the Commission's most important credit scheme was concerned.

The production of tobacco in the vicinity of Valle Nacional dates from the mid-1870's. Attracted by the favorable foreign investment laws of the Díaz regime and by the similarities between the Mexican tierra caliente and the tobacco regions of Cuba, several Spanish-owned firms from that island were drawn to the basin. After a few years of exploratory planting, these firms decided on the Valle Nacional, a valley some 20 miles long cut into the base of the Sierra by the river of the same name (Map 9), as the most promising location. Land was obtained from the indigenous Chinantec Indians by various means—some legal, others not—and production was started on a small scale.

The choice proved a happy one. The valley's climate and fertile alluvial soils proved ideal for the high quality Black Havana cigar leaf introduced from Cuba. A premium market in England, France, and the Netherlands was soon attracted, and within a decade Valle Nacional had become world renowned. Its Black Havana was awarded a first prize and gold medal at the Paris International Exposition in 1900, and by 1908 some 30 large plantations, almost all of them owned by Spaniards, were operating in the area. The value of their annual output, 98 per cent of it exported, has been estimated at be-tweeen six and seven million pesos, after adjustment for the peso's reduced real value, roughly 12 times that reported in the 1950 Census for the crop of the entire basin (1, pp. 1, 9).

But Valle Nacional's most prosperous period was in some respects also its worst. Almost from the start the area suffered from an acute shortage of labor. The indigenous Chinantecs proved poor workers and, once their land was lost, melted almost to a man into the surrounding hills. To take their place, the planters turned to importing contract laborers from the more populous parts of the country, with the understanding that they would stay at their jobs for a stated period. The deterioration of this system into a vicious form of debt servitude has been described by John K. Turner (14, p. 71):

> Some laborers tried to jump their contracts, and the planters used force to compel them to stay. The advance money and the cost of transportation was looked upon as a debt which the laborer could be compelled to work out. From this it was only a step to so ordering the conditions of labor that the laborer could under no circumstances ever hope to get free. In time Valle Nacional became a word of horror with the working people of all Mexico.

They refused to go there for any price. So the planters felt compelled to tell them they were going to take them somewhere else. From this it was only a step to playing the workman false all round, to formulating a contract not to be carried out, but to help get the laborer into the toils. Finally, from this it was only a step to forming a business partnership with the government, whereby the police power should be put into the hands of the planters to help them carry on a traffic in slaves.

The planters do not call their slaves slaves. They call them contract laborers. I call them slaves because the moment they enter Valle Nacional they become the personal property of the planter and there is no law or government to protect them. . . . The planter buys his slave for a given sum. Then he works him at will, feeds or starves him to suit himself, places armed guards over him day and night, beats him, pays him no money, kills him, and the laborer has no recourse.

If one can believe all of Turner's pamphleteering account of his visit there in 1908—and certainly the folklore of the Mexican Revolution has it that one can—conditions became so bad in Valle Nacional that fully nine of every ten contract laborers sent there never returned home; many were literally worked to death within a year of their arrival. But whether things really degenerated to such a point, it seems clear that tobacco cultivation proved highly profitable. Turner quotes the manager of one of the tobacco firms to the effect that to produce tobacco of similar quality cost less than half as much in the valley as in Cuba (*14*, pp. 67, 101).

But in spite of and to some extent because of the reliance on "slave" labor, the profits of the Valle Nacional planters were short lived. Tobacco is quite demanding on soil nutrients, and after years of continuous cropping the fertility of the valley's soils began to decline. Yields, which had once averaged over 1.5 tons per hectare, dropped to about a ton. Despite promising experiments with fertilizers, some of the planters thought they saw an easier solution. Rather than continue with Black Havana leaf, they persuaded their colleagues that with the higher-yielding but poorer-quality "Tlapacoyan" variety their returns could be maintained at no additional expense. During the first year (about 1910) Tlapacoyan was tried, this proved the case. Buyers accepted the new leaf without a murmur. But the following year they refused to buy. By the time the planters realized their mistake, forces beyond their control had intervened. World war in Europe cut off their market, while at home the fall of the Díaz regime spelled the end of their labor supply. With neither markets nor labor, the industry quickly collapsed, and by 1920 Valle Nacional was once again the home of subsistence Chinantec farmers.

Although some small cultivators continued to grow tobacco during the intervening years, production did not begin again in earnest until the more turbulent phase of the post-Revolutionary period had passed. By the early 1930's several of the old firms (or their successors) had resumed operations—but as buyers and processors, not producers. As such, they performed a dual function in the industry's revised make-up. For the peasants who now controlled production, tobacco was necessarily a secondary crop. Mostly semi-subsistence growers using traditional methods to cultivate two or three hectares each year, their poverty dictated that the greater part of their clearings be given over to corn and the other crops needed to satisfy their personal requirements. But provided they were able to obtain enough credit to meet the crop's heavy production outlays (chiefly for labor), an acre or two of tobacco offered an attractive source of cash income, especially since it would be grown during the winter season when land and labor would otherwise be idle.[9] Here the tobacco houses came into the picture — through the advance-purchase system described earlier. Through a chain of trader-intermediaries, the firms undertook to make the necessary funds available in exchange for the right to buy up the crop at previously determined prices.

But the return of the tobacco houses should not be taken to mean that the industry revived to anything like its former importance. Too much had changed for that. The small producers were considerably

[9] As in Cuba, tobacco in Valle Nacional is grown during the winter season in order to take advantage of the cooler temperatures and lower rainfall. Typically, the seedbeds are planted in August and September, to be followed by transplanting in November. Some three or four months later, in February and March, the leaves are harvested.

less efficient than the plantations they had replaced, and both the domestic and foreign tobacco markets had changed fundamentally. No longer was the dark, strong cigar leaf of Valle Nacional, particularly the poorer grades to which it had been permitted to degenerate, in great demand. Foreign buyers had become totally disillusioned and had found new sources of supply; while the domestic market, which by then favored the light, mild tobaccos used in cigarette manufacture, had come to depend chiefly on new centers of production in the state of Nayarit. But most important of all was the fact that the downward trend in yields had not been halted. After nearly 50 years of exploitive agriculture, Valle Nacional had become a marginal producer.

The next 20 years were years of regression. For this, the tobacco houses cannot be absolved from blame (*1*, pp. 2, 9). Once the new position of the industry in the valley was fully appreciated, they apparently wrote off the area as a possible source of quality tobacco. At Valle Nacional, the general disadvantages to the borrower inherent in the advance-purchase system were allowed to become particularly pronounced. In 1952/53, the earliest season for which any quantitative information is available, the growers did not receive their advances until October or November, although work had begun in August, and then were paid at the rate of only 770 pesos per hectare (*1*, p. 10). When compared with the estimated direct costs of making a crop in that year, and given the level of yields and prices then prevalent, the following picture emerges:

	Pesos per hectare
Estimated direct outlays[10]	1,550
Average gross return[11]	1,850
Apparent profit	300

Confronted with a loan quota that would cover only half his expected outlays, and faced with the prospect of a net return exclusive of overhead costs of only 300 pesos per hectare, the peasant's hand was

---

[10] Based on a wage of six pesos per day for hired labor, and broken down as follows (*1*, pp. 7–8) : Land preparation (including clearing) — 445 pesos; planting and field care — 460 pesos; harvesting, air-curing, and packing — 645 pesos.

[11] Based on an average yield of 575 kilograms (50 arrobas) and a price of 37 pesos per arroba.

forced. Having only the most primitive of implements at his command, he could introduce no practices that would lead to an increase in yield. Instead, he could only try to lower his unit outlays, accept the resultant reduction in yields and quality (both of which depend heavily on the care given the plant), and attempt to maintain his gross returns by less intensive cultivation.

In this manner, the position of tobacco as a cash crop in Valle Nacional, tenuous enough to begin with, was allowed to become progressively less secure. More and more pressed for funds, the growers gave their crops less and less attention. The buyers responded by offering lower and lower prices. By the early 1950's the industry was in a truly sorry state. Yields, which 20 years previously had averaged about 750 kilograms per hectare, had dropped to 575;[12] quality had reached the point where it literally could fall no further; and prices had declined to such an extent that the growers could expect to receive no more than the equivalent of 18 U.S. cents for a pound of their product (37 pesos per arroba of 11.5 kilograms) (*12*, p. 33; *1*, p. 10). Small wonder that when the Commission first became interested in the region, it found tobacco production steadily declining, and more and more growers abandoning any pretense of commercial participation.

The Approach and the Experience

The Commission became involved in Valle Nacional in 1953, when a section of the new Ciudad Alemán–Oaxaca highway was pushed into the valley. As work progressed, there seems to have been a decision by the Commission, undoubtedly influenced by Valle Nacional's associations with the Revolution, that, once opened up, the area should be made into something of a showplace. The construction of schools, sanitary works, and other physical improvements was promptly begun; and when, in early 1954, a committee representing the tobacco growers petitioned for aid, they alone among the many groups in the basin who had done so, received a promise of immediate assistance.

---

[12] In Nayarit, by way of contrast, yields in 1949/50 averaged 1,150 kilograms per hectare (*8*, p. 92).

The simplicity of the Valle Nacional scheme reflects the speed with which the Commission endeavored to make good this promise. A preliminary survey brought out the fact that only through a revolutionary upturn in quality and yields could the industry hope to get back on its feet, and that both technical assistance and a liberalized system of credit were urgently needed. It was first ordered that a program incorporating both aspects be started during the 1954/55 growing season. Those assigned responsibility for technical questions, however, freely confessed that their knowledge of both tobacco and local conditions was then far too inadequate for the recommendation of any cultural changes. It was therefore decided that the services of a tobacco specialist should be obtained, and that no attempt should be made to alter the prevailing methods of production until he had completed at least one round of experiments. In the meantime, however, the Commission should go ahead with the credit phase. Hence the significance of credit during the three years that the scheme was permitted to function. Not until April 1957 did the specialist submit his recommendations; a few months later the venture at Valle Nacional was drastically cut back along with the Commission's other lending operations.

The features of the credit experiment at Valle Nacional were significant chiefly because of the degree to which they departed from those of the advance-purchase system. In effect, the Commission set out to bridge the gap between advance purchase and credit practices as they prevail in more developed areas, and this above all called for the exclusion of the trader-intermediaries from the lending and marketing chain. Unlike the tobacco houses before it, the Commission lent directly to the growers. Terms were greatly liberalized. Instead of advancing only enough to cover a portion of the growers' cost, loan quotas were equated fully to expected outlays, with the first disbursements timed to coincide with the beginning of operations in August.[13] In addition, the growers were organized into marketing cooperatives

---

[13] The basic quota was set at 1,600 pesos per hectare; but since a grower's cash requirements varied with the area he planted (the smaller the area the more work he was able to do himself), the amount actually loaned per hectare varied considerably, and was usually well below this quota.

to enable them to sell directly to the buyers. All this of course had marked welfare implications; it was anticipated, however, that the modest interest charge of 9 per cent would enable the Commission to recover the expenses of its small local staff.

The elimination of the trader-intermediaries from the credit chain was a bold step. Their presence had not been without justification. As with semi-subsistence growers the world over, the Valle Nacional peasants were in a position to offer little guarantee that their loans would be repaid other than that of their personal skill and integrity. These, runs the argument in favor of advance purchase, a local man would be best able to assess, and who here would be a more logical choice than the local trader? In addition to coming into almost daily contact with the growers of his territory, the trader could bring economic pressure to bear, which offered unique insurance that the loans would be used for the purposes intended. Without such control, some peasants would probably make no attempt to repay. But was there not a fallacy here? Was the year-after-year need for such control sufficient to justify the discounts (of up to 25 per cent or more) that the traders took for their services? Once introduced to the lender and proved reliable, would not the borrower be at pains to protect the reputation upon which his cash income depended? This, in effect, the Commission set out to test. Though its loans called for crop liens and monthly inspections, in reality they were secured by the good names of the borrowers.

On the whole, the initial results were quite promising (*12*, Table 8; *11*, p. 169; *10*, p. 666):

Cropping cycle	Borrowers	Area (*hectares*)	Total loaned (*pesos*)	Total recovered (*pesos*)
1954/55	326	414	762,198	762,198
1955/56[14]	399	582	663,951	609,386

During the first season, 1954/55, the Commission financed about half of the valley's tobacco, some 414 hectares operated by 326 smallholders and ejidatarios. Production proceeded smoothly, with favorable weather resulting in an average yield slightly higher than normal,

[14] Includes Ojitlán and Playa Vicente.

604 kilograms per hectare. After some difficulty (the nature of which is discussed below), the crop was sold directly to a buying house at an average price of 46.60 pesos per arroba, roughly 10 pesos more than the trader-intermediaries were paying. The Commission not only recovered the entire extent of its loans; net returns to the growers were estimated at an unheard-of 1,000 pesos per hectare. An auspicious beginning indeed (9, p. 693; 3, pp. 1–2).

These results were so encouraging that the program was enlarged the following year. Impressed by the profits of their colleagues at Valle Nacional, several producer groups in Ojitlán and Playa Vicente (about 30 miles distant to the north and east, respectively) petitioned for inclusion. This increased the number of co-operating producers to almost 400 and the area under cultivation to 582 hectares. Again, the outcome was favorable, though not as spectacularly so as in 1954/55. Tobacco is highly sensitive to abnormal weather, with vagaries in rainfall especially almost always reducing yields. Though this is generally a minor problem in the basin because the crop is grown during the dry season on residual moisture, 1955/56 proved one of the exceptions. Abnormally high rainfall during the early winter so weakened the leaves that yields were cut almost in half— to 327 kilograms. Partly because the crop was eventually sold for an average of 50 pesos per arroba, however, this by no means meant huge losses. Of some 664,000 pesos advanced, the growers had failed to repay only 55,000 by the year's end, a very modest amount in view of the circumstances (10, p. 666).

But promising as these initial results were insofar as the main theme of the credit experiment was concerned, they should not be taken as suggesting that when it was curtailed in 1957 the Valle Nacional venture was well on its way toward unqualified success. Up to then the scheme had been little more than a holding operation: only through a sharp improvement in quality and yields could a permanent change for the better be expected, and this hinged on the companion program of research and technical aid. The outlook for this program was none too promising.

Basic to this conclusion is the fact that successful marketing of tobacco depends heavily on the good will of the buyers and processors. This is particularly true in the case of a new leaf, regardless of whether it represents an improvement in quality. It is no accident that most of the world's tobacco is grown in areas which have been developed in close cooperation with at least one manufacturer. With definite end-products in mind, the processor can and will buy only if he is certain that the new leaf will fit into his product, and that regular and sufficient supplies will continue to be forthcoming. This calls, if not for prearrangement, certainly for some sort of tacit understanding between the growers and the processors.

At Valle Nacional the Commission had laid the foundation for neither. Insofar as can be ascertained, its people on the spot made few attempts to convince the established buyers and processors of the desirability of the credit operation and to enlist their cooperation in a determined drive to revitalize the industry. They seem instead to have assumed almost completely the role of the peasants' protectors, thereby alienating the firms and individuals to whom the crop had to be sold. The reaction of the buyers was predictable. In both 1954/55 and 1955/56, considerable difficulty was experienced in finding buyers for the tobacco the Commission had financed. The principal processor, which previously had financed and purchased about two-thirds of the valley's output, made no attempt to conceal its distrust of the Commission's "real" objectives, leaving only a few small firms and speculators with whom its growers could deal. This situation came to a head in 1957. During the previous two seasons the Commission had closely supervised the selling operations of the producers' cooperatives, ensuring that all contracts were legitimate. This supervision was relaxed in 1957, with the result that the greater part of the crop came under the control of a speculator who proved devoid of ethics. Though the crop itself was promising, the upshot of a series of fraudulent transactions and legal maneuvers was a serious loss to both the growers and the Commission: of a credit of 920,000 pesos, only 606,000 pesos were recovered.

CITATIONS

1 Roxana Arce Ybarra, "El problema del tabaco en el Valle Nacional" (Comisión del Papaloapan, July 1954, unpublished).

2 "Colonias controladas por la Comisión" (Comisión del Papaloapan, April 1956, unpublished).

3 Juan Garcia Sandoval, "Informe relativo a las aspectos más importantes de cultivo, producción y habilitación del tabaco en la cuenca del Papaloapan" (Comisión del Papaloapan, June 1955, unpublished).

4 Instructions, dated April 23, 1956, from Jefatura de Obras Bombeo, Río Tonto, to the Administrative Councils of the Los Naranjos colonies (Comisión del Papaloapan, unpublished).

5 Elías Kesselbrenner, "Estudio de gran visión de la zona comprendida entre el arroyo Hondo y el arroyo Estanzuela, municipios de Tierra Blanca y Cosamaloapan, estado de Veracruz" (Comisión del Papaloapan, 1949, unpublished).

6 Alfonso Marquez L., "Informe del estudio agrológico detallado de una parte de la primera unidad agrícola del distrito de riego 'Presidente Miguel Alemán,' Veracruz" (Comisión del Papaloapan, 1951, unpublished).

7 "Memoria de la dirección de fomento agropecuario y crédito" (Comisión del Papaloapan, 1959, unpublished).

8 Mexico, Sec. Econ., Dir. Gen. Estad., *Tercer censo agrícola ganadero y ejidal, 1950. Resumen general* (1956).

9 Mexico, Sec. Rec. Hid., *Informe de labores de la secretaría de recursos hidraulicos del 1°. de septiembre de 1954 al 31 de agosto de 1955.*

10 Mexico, Sec. Rec. Hid., *Informe de labores de la secretaría de recursos hidraulicos del 1°. de septiembre de 1955 al 31 de agosto de 1956.*

11 Fernando Rosenzweig Hernandez, "Crédito agrícola en el Papaloapan," *El trimestre económico*, XXIV, April–June 1957.

12 Fernando Rosenzweig Hernandez, "El programa de crédito agrícola de la Comisión del Papaloapan" (Comisión del Papaloapan, March 1957, unpublished).

13 *Tiempo* (México, D. F.), Mar. 21, 1947.

14 J. K. Turner, *Barbarous Mexico* (Chicago, 1910).

Chapter 8

GUIDEPOSTS FOR THE FUTURE

One comes away from a study of the Papaloapan Project with two main conclusions. The first is that it would be a serious mistake for the Mexican government to keep the development program in its present state of abeyance. This is not to minimize the significance of errors the Commission has made, but to recognize that in spite of them a noteworthy move has been made in the direction of sustained regional growth. In a country like Mexico this counts for much.

The second major conclusion is that the meager accomplishments of the Commission's agricultural projects should stand as a warning to the difficulties of agricultural development in the tropics. Although evaluation along the usual cost-benefit lines is ruled out by the paucity of reliable statistics, it is clear that the communications, flood control, and other programs concerned with building up the basin's economic infrastructure have yielded substantial results, whereas the agricultural program has not. From this fact and from the specific experiences of the pilot agricultural schemes, it would seem possible to infer several lessons that can help to point the way to a sounder course of action in the future, both in the basin and in Mexico's other humid tropical areas.

Consider first the pilot schemes, especially Los Naranjos and Michapan. Here the policy followed by the Commission was one of extreme paternalism, the settlers having been supplied with complete farms-in-being as well as follow-up technical and financial aid. We have seen that the outcome was anything but auspicious. In neither zone was the groundwork laid for successful settlement, despite initial outlays approximating $2,000 per family and four years of supervised operation.

What lessons can be drawn from this experience? The most basic, it would seem, relates to the limitations of what we have here called

153

the paternalistic approach in a newly opened and therefore little understood tropical area. That a successful program of this type requires a substantial backlog of knowledge of local conditions was clearly demonstrated at Los Naranjos and Michapan.

D. E. M. Fiennes, who served as a land-settlement officer in Malaya and West Africa, has concluded that if government is to supply more than a bare minimum of aid, a sound program of colonization must pass through three stages: an experimental stage, in which answers are sought to questions about which no information is available; a pilot stage, in which plans are tested on a modest, controlled scale; and a final stage, in which full-scale implementation of approved plans is attempted (*1*, pp. 37–38). At Los Naranjos and Michapan the Commission bypassed the first stage completely; indeed, it might be said that the Commission plunged immediately into the last stage. Before any preliminary experiments were carried out to determine the optimum size of holding, the local suitability of alternative crops, and the types of machinery best adapted to the various tasks, the colonies were laid out and settlers accepted.

Colonizing a new area is always a risky operation. However, it is particularly so when technical innovations are contemplated. They must necessarily add to the already complex human variables involved and there is little evidence to support a supposition that practices which have proved suitable in one environment can be transposed without modification into another. The Commission assumed the opposite when it attempted to introduce a whole new system of semi-mechanized production into its colonies. If the tractor had revolutionized temperate-zone agriculture, would it not almost by its mere presence do the same in the tropics?

This type of reasoning, combined with the absence of established centers of sedentary cultivation elsewhere in the interfluvial plains, resulted in a disastrous situation. The Commission's field men, instead of being able to introduce combinations of crops and cultural practices whose worth under local conditions had been demonstrated, were obliged to formulate many of their plans and instructions around little more than conjecture. Mistakes were inevitable. Inappropriate crops were selected, unsuitable machinery was chosen, ill-advised planting dates were designated. With unanticipated complications year after year keeping incomes at levels well below those expected, the Commission was unable to offer its colonists the prospect of a way of life appreciably better than the one they had left.

The main point, of course, is that the Commission left far too much to chance. The essence of the paternalistic approach to development is that close direction and heavy investment will make possible high immediate returns. But unless there are firm technical grounds for such returns, the approach loses all validity.

In contrast to the colonization schemes, the experience of the Commission's credit operation at Valle Nacional was not unpromising. Here the Commission set out to test the feasibility of direct governmental intervention to facilitate the transition from advance purchase to more equitable credit and marketing practices. Could not government perform a real service by developing a class of peasants worthy of greater trust and then by introducing them to lenders? The early results suggested an affirmative answer. Out of almost 1.55 million pesos lent during the first two years of the scheme, losses amounted to less than 4 per cent.

The principal lesson of Valle Nacional, however, stems not from this auspicious beginning but from the events of the third year. Whereas the Commission had closely supervised the marketing operations of its growers during the first two seasons, it relaxed this guidance during the third for reasons that are not altogether clear. Without the advice and assistance of a sympathetic officialdom, the growers quickly fell prey to the manipulations of unscrupulous interests. Losses were so heavy that it is doubtful whether the scheme would have been continued in any circumstances.

Combined with the results of the colonization schemes, this experience at Valle Nacional reinforces the frequently overlooked precept that economic growth in a newly opened area hinges on more than inputs of capital. As the Commission painfully discovered, an abundance of capital, desirable though it may be, cannot make up for inadequate knowledge and a shortage of skilled personnel. Is the backlog of technical evidence sufficient to justify a particular course of action? Will it fit harmoniously into the existing institutional setting? Are an adequate number of trained personnel available to administer it? If these and similar questions cannot be answered affirmatively, to proceed before they can be, no matter how heavy the capitalization, is to court waste and a strong possibility of failure.

In this connection, it would appear that agricultural programs of the type employed by the Commission suffer from two immediate and major disadvantages relative to other means of promoting development in the humid tropics of Mexico. The first arises from the fact that such programs are directly concerned with human beings. Accordingly, they require a larger number of technicians to assist a given group of people than would, say, a road-building scheme, and therefore make less efficient use of a pool of skilled manpower that is still small. The second disadvantage is attested to by the sharp contrast between the results of the Commission's agricultural activities and its other programs: unlike most professional skills, the agricultural arts as applied under temperate conditions have only limited relevance in the tropics. Accordingly, Mexico's capabilities with regard to tropical agriculture are even more restricted than would at first appear to be the case.

This suggests, of course, that for the immediate future an important comparative advantage in the field of Mexican tropical development lies in the building of roads, dams, schools, and other social overheads. It is not to argue, however, that these works should be pressed to the exclusion of programs specifically concerned with agriculture, or that the concept of balanced investment should be downgraded. Rather, it would seem a clear call for current and future investment in agriculture to be shifted away from complex schemes involving direct government participation in the day-to-day activities of the growers and moved increasingly in the direction of research, experimentation, and technical education. Had this call been equally clear to the Commission 16 years ago, the Papaloapan Project would without a doubt stand today as a truly major milestone in the economic development of Mexico.

CITATION

1 D. E. M. Fiennes, "Land Settlement in Asia and Africa," *Colonial Development*, II, Summer 1956.

APPENDIX NOTE

APPENDIX NOTE

Census Statistics for the Papaloapan Basin

Because certain difficulties were involved in compiling a set of comparable basic data around which to build a description of the population and agricultural economy of the Papaloapan basin, the census statistics presented in Chapters 3 and 4 of this study warrant a word of explanation and caution. As yet there are no census-type data for the basin per se, and iti s unlikely that there will be for some time to come. For the present the decennial Censuses of Population and Agriculture for the entire country represent the only available sources. Unfortunately, the political entities for which the data in these censuses have been tabulated and summarized coincide neither with the basin's sub-regions nor with the area as a whole. Regroupings and compromises were therefore required if statistics of any meaning were to be prepared.

The basic political unit for which census data are normally tabulated in Mexico is the *municipio* (municipality), an entity corresponding roughly to the county in the United States. The basin embraces all or parts of 246 municipios, 33 of them in the state of Puebla, 60 in Veracruz, and no less than 153 in Oaxaca. Because of the vast number of tiny municipios included in Oaxaca, however, the data in the Agricultural Censuses for this state are published only for *ex-distritos,* groupings of municipios based on the political subdivisions set up during the Díaz era. For Oaxaca, therefore, the ex-distrito is the smallest unit for which all census data are available. Eleven ex-distritos fall totally or partially within the Oaxaca portion of the basin.

The arbitrary criterion employed in determining whether for statistical purposes a given municipio or ex-distrito should be regarded as a part of the basin was the percentage of its total area falling within the region. Those entities with more than 50 per cent of their area in the basin were considered as being wholly included, while those with less than half were excluded. The "statistical basin" resulting from this compromise is shown in Map 11. It will be noted that the distortions introduced are not of major importance. In fact, with respect to both area and population, the basin and its statistical counterpart are quite comparable. The "statistical basin" embraces an area only 72 square miles larger than the basin itself, and in 1950 contained only about 25,000 more people (this latter figure was derived from detailed adjustments of census data preparable only for the number of inhabitants).

The same procedure was followed in arriving at the statistical counterparts of the basin's major sub-regions. Here again an examination of Map 11 reveals that the result is quite serviceable, although in certain instances somewhat less satisfactory. The most obvious distortion is an overstatement of the area (and population) of the lower basin at the expense of the upper, a situation that grew out of the necessity to include the vast ex-distrito of

159

MAP 11.—PAPALOAPAN BASIN: RELATION BETWEEN
NATURAL AND STATISTICAL REGIONS

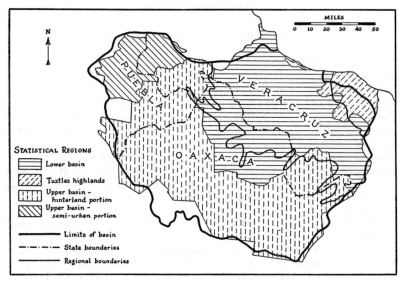

Tuxtepec in the lower basin in its entirety. Another shortcoming is the inclusion within the Tuxtlas highlands of an area of almost equal size lying outside the basin portion of this region. But these faults are relatively minor, and once borne in mind need not detract from the usefulness of the data.

The following is an enumeration by sub-region of the 82 municipios and 8 ex-distritos which for statistical purposes are considered as falling within the Papaloapan basin:

LOWER BASIN

Oaxaca (ex-distrito).—Tuxtepec.

Veracruz (municipios). — Acula, Alvarado, Amatitlán, Cosamaloapan, Chacaltianguis, Hueyapan de Ocampo, Ignacio de la Llave, Ixmatlahuacán, Lerdo de Tejada, Otatitlán, Saltabarranca, San Juan Evangelista, Santiago Tuxtla, Tesechoacán, Tierra Blanca, Tlacojalpan, Tlacotalpan, Tlalixcoyan, Tuxtilla.

UPPER BASIN—HINTERLAND PORTION

Oaxaca (ex-distritos). — Coixtlahuaca, Cuicatlán, Choápan, Ixtlán de Juarez, Mixe, Teotitlán, Villa Alta.

Puebla (municipios).—Ajalpan, Altepexi, Caltepec, Coxcatlán, Coyomeapan, Eloxochitlán, San Antonio Cañada, San Gabriel Chilac, San José Miahuatlán, San Sebastián Tlacotepec, Vicente Guerrero, Zinacatepec, Zoquitlán.

Veracruz (municipios).—Astacinga, Atlahuilco, Mixtla de Altamirano, Playa Vicente, Reyes, Tehuipango, Tenejapa de Mata, Texhuacán, Tlaquilpa, Xoxocotla, Zongolica.

UPPER BASIN—SEMI-URBAN PORTION

Puebla (municipios).—Atzizintla, Chalchicomula, Chapulco, Esperanza, Morelos Cañada, Nicolás Bravo, Santiago Miahuatlán, Tehuacán, Tepango de López, Tlacotepec, Yehualtepec, Palmar de Bravo.

Veracruz (municipios). — Acultzingo, Amatlán de los Reyes, Aquila, Atzacan, Coetzala, Camerino Z. Mendoza, Córdoba, Fortín, Huiloapan, Ixhuatlancillo, Ixtazoquitlán, La Perla, Magdalena, Maltrata, Mariano Escobeda, Naranjal, Nogales, Orizaba, Rafaél Delgado, San Andrés Tenejapa, Soledad Atzompa, Tenango de Río Blanco, Tequila, Tlilapan.

TUXTLAS HIGHLANDS

Veracruz (municipios).—Angel R. Cabada, Catemaco, San Andrés Tuxtla.

INDEX

INDEX